The what it cost the day before yesterday book

The what it cost the da

-from 1850 to the present day

by Dr Harold Priestley

65

before yesterday book

Kenneth Mason

ISBN 085937 0828

Published by Kenneth Mason, Homewell, Havant, Hampshire

Printed in Great Btitain by Coasbyprint Limited,Claybank Road, Portsmouth, Hants and designed by Sadlergraphics.

Contents

To my two young nephews
Ian and David Peacock
who always want to know

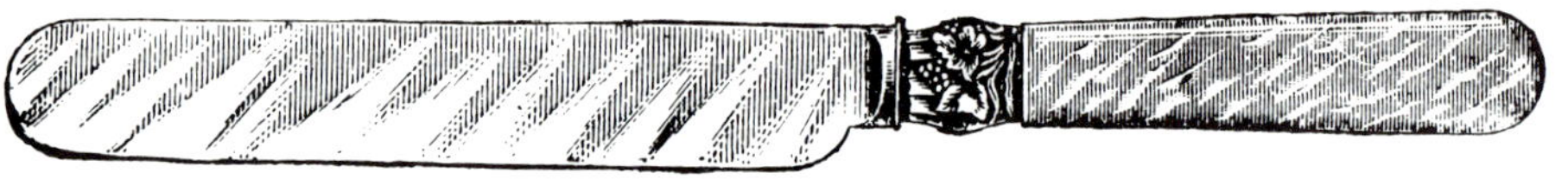

Acknowledgements

I would like to thank the following for much of the information supplied for this book: The Ministry of Agriculture Fisheries and Food, The National Coal Board, The Electricity Council, The Brewers' Society, British Gas, The North Thames Gas Board, The Department of Health and Social Security, The Herring Industry Board, The Milk Marketing Board, The Post Office, The Potato Marketing Board, The Television Licensing Organisation, The Automobile Association, The British Egg Information Service, The Dairy Trade Federation, The Institute of Gas Engineers, The National Dairy Council, John Player and Sons, The Headmaster – The City of London School, The Headmistress – City of London School for Girls, *The Times, The Daily Mail, The Bradford Daily Telegraph and Argus, The Grocer, The Meat Trades Journal.*

Thanks also to the Librarian and Staff of the London Borough of Newham (especially to Mrs E Taylor and Mr Frank Sainsbury); The Librarian and Staff of the Borough of Southend-on-Sea, The Librarian and Staff of the County of Essex Libraries, Mrs Ann Warren, Mr R C Chandler, Mr J Downer, Mr F Estall, Mr E G Green, Mr Will H Maile, Mr A Rushfirth, Mr E Purdy, Mr Fred Tombs and numerous other friends, correspondents and neighbours who have supplied many mail order catalogues, have provided their own personal recollections and many old receipts for goods and services.

Finally, my wife for help in so many ways including laborious transcription from journals and microfilms.

A washing machine of the 1890s. Prices from £2.33.

For the child of 1895
– a tricycle horse with
rubber tyre wheels at £1.37

Introduction

The twentieth century has seen more changes than any other in the amount of goods which the pound sterling can buy. There was a time within living memory when a working-class family could live quite comfortably on a payment of less than that sum for all weekly groceries, when the wages of the working man were usually less than £2, his rent not more than five to six shillings a week (25 to 30 new pence) and a joint of beef costing £1.25 a pound or more today could be bought for ten old pence (4¼ p).

Wages, like prices were, at the beginning of the period with which we deal in this book (1851) a mere fraction of what they are now. There was no state retirement pension nor any general government pension scheme, no unemployment or state sickness benefit. The destitute were taken to the workhouses or paid small sums of a few shillings a week by the parish Overseers of the Poor.

On the other hand, life was much more simple. There was none of the articles which are now considered almost necessities by the average householder – the car, the vacuum cleaner, the refrigerator, the deep freeze, the washing machine, the radiogram, stereo, television set and many of the household gadgets we see advertised.

Although there were rises in prices during war years (1914–1918 and 1939–1945) and sometimes considerable fluctuations in other decades, rapid inflation did not come in Great Britain until after the second world war, reaching its alarming climax in 1977. By that time the general public had become increasingly concerned by the escalating costs which had only partly been met by wage rises owing to repeated efforts to implement pay policies. Not only the Government, but trade unions and employers strove, sometimes in agreement, sometimes separately to achieve some sort of wage-price parity by limited rises in pay and by control of prices. At that time the goal of the Government was single figure inflation, that is, less than ten pence in the pound per year.

In view of all this it has seemed worthwhile to draw up a series of tables showing the actual retail prices of some staple goods and services from ancient times to the present day. This present volume deals with the more recent period 1850 to now. This has been done in periods of ten years from 1851 to 1970, with the exception of the decades of the two world wars in which they rose more rapidly. In the years from 1971 onwards Great Britain experienced what was then known as galloping inflation (though by no means as 'galloping' as in some other countries) due largely to the general world rise in prices. For this decade each year has therefore been treated separately.

The book has been divided into three sections: 1851 - 1914, 1915 - 1970, and 1971 - 1978. Each section has its own set of tables and each of the first two its own appendix giving prices of articles which are too infrequently mentioned to be put into the tables.

There are omissions. In some cases it has been found impossible up to the present at least, to quote costs of certain commodities and services because of scarcity of information. In others there are contradictions and a good deal of investigation may still have to be done in journals or whatever business records become available.

This lack of data occurs mainly when one organisation gives way to another, where concerns have merged, where public bodies or the Government have taken over particular industries or services. Thus records of earlier concerns have been filed away, deposited or lost, and to bring them to light may demand both time and labour. This book may be considered as being the starting-point for a project which could in the end cover the whole period of British history as far back as the Norman Conquest and possibly earlier.

Absolute accuracy is impossible. Certain commodities such as coal varied greatly in the price charged not only at the pithead but also in all parts of the country owing to differing costs of transport. Others, especially foodstuffs such as eggs, apples and potatoes varied in price with the changing seasons or the weather. Certain cuts of meat were cheaper than others. Tea and petrol were subject to duties which were altered in amount from one decade to another. Prices of houses were higher in the south-east than elsewhere. Clothing, footwear and other items were sold in widely differing qualities. Each gas and electricity undertaking had its own tariffs, and these became more complicated in more recent years.

Hence we cannot quote average prices for most goods. Suits may have varied from £15 to £75 in the same year; dining-room suites from £30 to £300. Therefore the compromise arrived at in these tables is not an average. All we can do in drawing them up is to ask, 'What was the price at which goods of at least medium quality could

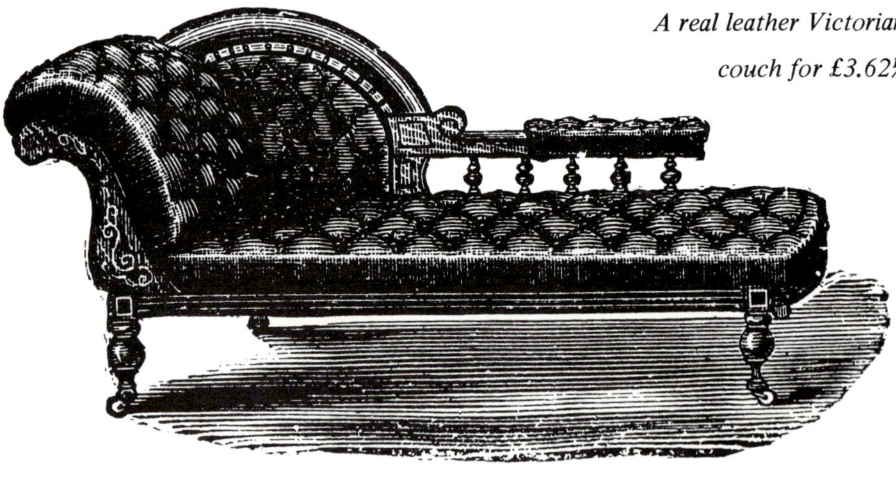

A real leather Victorian couch for £3.62½

be bought?' The figures we give are what we would expect those who ran the working-class or lower middle-class family to pay, and some of the prices given may be sale prices. Thus we quote suits off-the-peg, underwear and separates, furniture and household goods made in bulk and advertised in mail order catalogues, journals and newspapers. Prices in successive tables may vary owing to differences in quality both of goods and services.

Only when we come to universals such as postage rates, motor tax, income tax levels, radio and TV licences and retirement pensions do we find uniformity over the whole country and this occurs in some cases mainly over the last half of the period under review.

To bring some order out of the many facts and figures, only one line has been quoted in the tables wherever possible, as for instance in railways, the cost of a single journey from London to Manchester, the cost of a therm of gas and a unit of electricity charged by a single concern or board, the cost of posting a letter etc. Three public schools have been chosen to provide samples of the fees charged, and only the *Times* and the *Daily Mail* from all the newspapers published. Where there are gaps in the tables the information has not so far been obtainable.

This is not a history of the cost of living, though some attempt has been made to match pay and prices, giving certain figures for wages over the period, of state retirement pensions since 1910 and the rate of income tax. These have been put together in an attempt to answer questions so often asked as to what proportion of their incomes our parents, grandparents and great grandparents paid for some of the goods they bought.

Through reading advertisements it is interesting to see how man's needs and fashions changed over the years, as certain articles passed out of use and others appeared. Gone are the days of the hip bath, the cholera belt and the moustache cup with its porcelain ledge. Boot polish has superseded the bar of blacking which needed so much spit and elbow-grease to get a shine. The gentleman dressing for dinner or a reception no longer dons a stiff detachable shirt-front or dickey, nor does his wife wear a camisole or his maiden aunt draw on a pair of knitted kneecaps against the cold. The magic lantern has been made obsolete by the moving, talking picture and the fountain pen and stylo pen have lost ground to the almost ubiquitous ballpoint. Even names of items have occasionally changed. What were once universally called false teeth are now dentures.

Among new commodities are all those which have been introduced as a result of modern invention and technology. These include all the household power-gadgets, stoves, cookers, kettles and refrigerators. With the passing of the years the rise in real incomes has created a phenomenal demand for the motor-car, whereas at one time it was only the well-off family who could sport a horse and trap. To all those we should add the lawn mower, the moveable greenhouse, garage and garden shed.

The same applies to services. Less than a century ago corns on the feet were trimmed, if you had a steady hand, with a cut-throat razor, if not, with the sandpaper on the side of a matchbox. Now we visit the chiropodist. In days when doctoring and dentistry cost money, bowels were kept open by doses of castor oil, brimstone and treacle or liquorice powder according to urgency. There were no school medical inspections and a milk tooth was taken out at home by tying a piece of thread round it and giving it a smart jerk.

In 1895 it was possible to go to a large store, test your own eyes in front of a chart and choose a suitable pair of steel-rimmed spectacles from a tray for 5p. In Woolworths in 1930 you could do the same for 2½p.

Especially since the last war there has been a mounting demand for more elaborate and distant holidays. Before 1914 a week at Brighton or Blackpool complete with rock, bathing-machines and pierrots was generally arranged privately at a boarding-house. Today a tourist organisation can take one anywhere in the world. It is interesting to note, too, that though the real craze for roller-skating started round about 1908, Harrods were selling roller-skates in 1895 at 35p a pair.

For all these reasons the three sets of tables differ slightly in content, some of the items appearing in the appendix of the first section being put into the tables in the second and third.

In 1971 the country changed over to decimal coinage, and we have now reached a point where to some young minds, pounds, shillings and pence are little known. For this reason most prices have been reduced to decimals. This presents certain difficulties; for instance, one new penny is only an approximate decimal value of the old 2½ pence and 4 new pence of the old 9½ pence, but we have to make the best of it. Moreover, whereas present statistical tables quote pennies and parts of pennies in decimal fractions, this book gives these to the nearest half or quarter for the benefit of some of the public, especially the elderly who are not able easily to juggle with decimals. For certain items such as postages and newspapers both the old and the decimal values, the latter to fifths of a new penny, are given. The figures for electricity after decimalisation in 1971 are taken from actual accounts and are transcribed direct in new pence and decimals of a penny per unit. The most detailed appendix is that to section 1 (1851–1914); the last section (1971–1978), which covers only eight years, has no appendix.

In compiling this book I have realised what great interest there is everywhere in how much things cost in former years. Neighbours have brought newspaper cuttings and numbers of old and current mail order catalogues; even school children have appeared with notes on scraps of paper.

It seems strange that up to the present there is so little available information. Official records do not take us far, but there must be a great deal to be found in various archives, store-rooms, old house journals, newspapers, magazines and all sorts of odd places, or, failing these, in the memories of older people.

We find that we are only at the beginning of what could be a fascinating and wide-ranging study, and we would welcome facts about prices in past days from any reader who may be able to fill out these columns or add interesting items to the appendices.

Harold Priestley 1979

1851 - 1914

The period may be divided roughly into three parts, the first two of about 25 years and the third of 14. Each of these shows a different trend from the one preceding it.

The thirties and forties of the last century saw rapid changes and successive financial crises in Great Britain. The constant panics which accompanied them brought many bank failures and to prevent these Sir Robert Peel's government in 1844 passed the Bank Charter Act. This measure, whose main provision was to limit the amount of notes that could be issued to no more than 14 million pounds more than the value of gold, silver and bullion held by the Bank of England, did much to stabilise banking, trade and prices.

In spite of this, the years between 1851 and 1873 saw a steady and substantial rise in prices, caused to some extent by what was happening abroad. The Crimean War of 1854 - 55 brought about a scarcity of certain goods; there was pressure on the Bank of England to create more currency, and the Bank Charter Act had to be suspended temporarily in 1857. The action of the United States in going over to a paper currency which could not be changed into gold, caused an influx of gold into Europe and an increase of unhealthy speculation. Then came the American Civil War of 1864–65 which stopped the export of cotton to Great Britain, causing manufacturers to search for supplies from Egypt, China and Brazil. These, paid for in gold, encouraged over-trading, more speculation and a crisis which had to be met by a second suspension of the Bank Charter Act. Prices being bound up to a large extent with the relationship between goods and the amount of money in circulation, the period between 1851 and 1873 saw a rise of some 25 per cent. This was, however, covered by a corresponding general rise in wages so that real wages rose considerably on what they had been at the beginning of the period.

Political events bring economic consequences. The Repeal of the Corn Laws in 1846 had allowed foreign corn into Great Britain free of duty. As long as the British farmer was not faced with severe competition things went well, but in the last quarter of the century, with the United States free from north-south enmity and Canada rapidly expanding towards the Pacific and developing its vast prairies into wheatlands, increasing amounts of corn came to be grown in the New World and was imported at cheaper rates than the British farmer could afford to produce it. This affected British agriculture and ultimately British trade and industry, bringing about widespread unemployment.

In 1871 the Franco-Prussian War ended with the unification of Germany into an empire, and brought about the formation of the Third French Republic. Up to this time Great Britain had been a step ahead of all other countries in industrial production and had been able to furnish the whole world with machinery and manufactured goods at a cheaper rate than any other country. From 1871 onwards, however, Germany in particular emerged as a powerful manufacturing and trading rival, the spearhead of competition with Britain not only in commerce, but towards the end of the century in the contest for colonies and military power. Capital which had once flowed into London began to find outlets on the Continent, in the United States and especially in varous parts of South America. The virtual trade monopoly which the British had once enjoyed gradually vanished, and people began to doubt the wisdom of the Free Trade policy brought in by Peel and Gladstone.

Thus in industry Great Britain experienced a fall in demand, a fall in prices as foreign goods came in, and a vast rise in unemployment which struck both at agriculture and industry. The result was that the employed worker, whose wages on the whole remained stationary, enjoyed a rather better standard of living than formerly, but industrial discontent increased among the lower-paid workers, and the

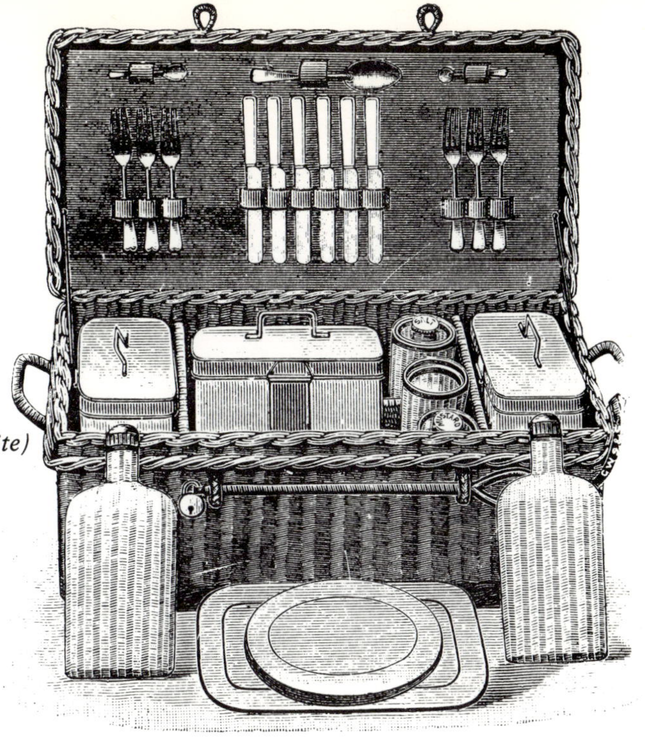

A Bluthner piano (opposite) from 61 to 300 guineas, and (right) a picnic basket for £2.35

unemployed, whose numbers rose at times up to a million and who had no state relief, suffered great hardship.

The tide began to turn in the nineties, and by the beginning of the new century markets had become more stable and prices began to rise again. This price rise up to 1900 was met by a gradual rise in wages which levelled off and remained stationary until 1914 so that in the early years of the 20th century real wages fell slowly.

At the same time industrial and commercial competition, especially between Great Britain and Germany, had given way to a rivalry for political and military power, a large increase in the German armed forces and a movement of all European powers to acquire colonies and dependencies, especially in Africa and the Far East. The old enemies, Germany and France, looked round for allies and out of the negotiations two armed camps emerged. These were the Triple Alliance of Germany, Austria and Italy and the Triple Entente of France, Russia and Great Britain. Three times in the early years of the century the powers reached the very brink of war. The fourth international crisis started with the assassination of the Archduke Franz Ferdinand of Austria at Sarajevo in Serbia on June 28 1914. Its sequel was the first World War of 1914–18.

From the time of the declaration of war on August 4, everything had to be sacrificed to the production of armaments and the support of the armed forces. Prices increased rapidly and by the time peace was signed in 1919, had doubled themselves.

FOOD DRINK TOBACCO	1851 – 60	1861 – 70
Bacon per lb	5p	5p
Beer per gallon	5p	5p
Bread 4lb loaf	3½p	3½p
Butter per lb	5½p	8p
Cheese per lb	4p	4p
Cigarettes	not available	1000 Turkish £3.75
Coffee per lb	5p	5p
Eggs per dozen	5p	5p
Meat – Beef	3p	3p
Mutton and Lamb	3½p	3p
Pork	4p	4p
Milk per pint	½p	¾p
Potatoes 14lb	2p	3p
Sugar per lb	1½p	1½p
Tea per lb	16½p	16½p (inc 5p duty)
Tobacco per oz	1p	1p

CLOTHING	1851 – 60	1861 – 70
Overcoat	£1.75	£1.75
Stockings	10p	10p
Suits	£1.12½	£1.25

FURNITURE	1851 – 60	1861 – 70
Bed double with mattress	£2.50	£2.50
Dining Table full size	£7.25	£8

1871 – 80	1881 – 90	1891 – 1900	1901 – 10	1910 – 14
5p	3½p	3p	3½p	5p
5p	5p	5p	6p	6p
3p	2½p	2p	2½p	2½p
8½p	6p	6p	6p	6p
4½p	3p	4p	5p	5p
100 Egyptian 25p	100 Egyptian 22½p	Wills Gold Flake 20 for 2p	Players' Medium 20 for 2p	20 for 3p
7½p	Best 8p	Ordinary 4p	6p	7p
5p	5p	5p	6p	5½p
4p	4p	4½p	5p	5p
4p	leg 5½p	4½p	4p	4p
4p	3p	3½p	3p	4p
¾p	¾p	½p	¾p	¾p
3p	3p	3p	3p	2½p
2p	¾p	¾p	1p	1p
15p	12p (inc . 1½p duty)	7p	8p	6½p
1p	1p	2p	2p	2½p

1871 – 80	1881 – 90	1891 – 1900	1901 – 10	1910 – 14
£2	£2	£2	£2	£2
12p	12½p	12½p	12p	12p
£1.50	£1.25	£1.40	£1.75	£1.90

1871 – 80	1881 – 90	1891 – 1900	1901 – 10	1910 – 14
£2.50	£2.75	£2.75	£2.75	£3
£8.50	£8.50	£8.50	£9	£9

HEAT & LIGHT	1851 – 60	1861 – 70
Coal per ton	86p (London)	£1 (London) Best £1.50
Electricity (SE England) per unit	NO SERVICES	
Gas	22p per 1000 cu ft (approx 4½p per therm)	22p per 1000
SERVICES		
Postage (inland letter)	1d (2/5p)	1d (2/5p)
Newspapers Daily Mail	NOT IN EXISTENCE	
Times	5d (2p) 1853 4d (1 3/5p) when tax abolished	1861 3d (1 1/5p)
Railway Fares London - Manchester 3rd Class Single	Parliamentary trains, each company running one a day at 1d (2/5p) per mile	1865 LNWR 9p per mile 75p
London Omnibus Fares (LGOC founded 1856)	HORSEDRAWN TRANSPORT FARES VARIED WITH FREQUENCY OF SERVICES 1866 ST JOHN'S WOOD - LONDON BRIDGE 5½m every 8 mins 6d ROYAL OAK - LONDON BRIDGE 5½m every 4 mins 5d	
TRANSPORT (private)		
Bicycle	SLOWLY DEVELOPING	
Family car	NOT AVAILABLE	
HOUSING		
Cost of 2 bedroom house	£225	£250
Rent per week working class house	27p	30p
INCOME		
Labourer's Wage per week	75p	75p
State Pension	NOT IN EXISTENCE	
INCOME TAX in £	Average 2½p (3 changes)	Average 2½p (5 changes)

1871 – 80	1881 – 90	1891 – 1900	1901 – 10	1910 – 14
£1.50	£1.05 best main	£1.15 Wallsend	£1.25	£1.25
SERVICES DEVELOPING		2½p	Lighting 1st hour 3p, then 3/5p Flat rate 2p Power 4/5p 1st hour then 3/5p	3p 2p 4/5p and 3/5p
22p per 1000	20p per 1000	20p per 1000	15p per 1000 (approx 3p per therm)	15p per 1000

1871 – 80	1881 – 90	1891 – 1900	1901 – 10	1910 – 14
1d (2/5p) to 1oz 2nd oz ½d (1/5p) more	1d to 1oz	1d to 1oz 1897 1d to 4oz	1d to 4oz	1d to 4oz
NOT IN EXISTENCE		May 4 1890 ½d (1/5p)	½d	½d
3d	3d	3d	3d	3d
PENNY - A - MILE SERVICES CONTINUED				
75p	75p	75p approx	75p approx	75p approx
(RAILWAY COMPANIES IN COMPETITION)				
MECHANICAL TRANSPORT DEVELOPING HORSES STILL USED 1888 CRICKLEWOOD - OXFORD CIRCUS 4½m every 30 mins 5d CHARING CROSS - KILBURN 4½m every 12 mins 4d				

1871 – 80	1881 – 90	1891 – 1900	1901 – 10	1910 – 14
Penny farthing £8 with gears £12	Safety bicycle £7.50	£10	£12	£12.50
NOT AVAILABLE		£200	Rover 8 hp 2 seater £200	£200

1871 – 80	1881 – 90	1891 – 1900	1901 – 10	1910 – 14
£250	£300	£300	£300	£350
30p	35p	35p	35p	40p

1871 – 80	1881 – 90	1891 – 1900	1901 – 10	1910 – 14
85p	90p	£1	£1.10	£1.30
NOT IN EXISTENCE				1909 25p
Average 3p (7 changes)	Average 3p (7 changes)	Average 3½p (4 changes)	Average 5½p (5 changes)	6p (no changes)

SIXTY PRIZE MEDALS AWAR
FRY'S
PURE
CONCENTRATED SOLUBLE
COCOA
Prepared by a new and special scientific process, securing extreme solubility, and developing the finest flavour of the Cocoa
PURE. EASILY DIGESTED.
ECONOMICAL.
J. S. FRY & SONS,
BRISTOL, LONDON & SYDNEY.

"Raised on it."

CLOTHING
corsets *15p*
petticoat *8p*
riding habit, to measure *£10.50*
shoes, elastic-sided *15p*
silk dress lengths *£1 per yard*
suit, lady's, serge *£1.12*

COST OF FIRST EDITIONS
Dickens Tale of two cities (1859) *37½p*
George Eliot Adam Bede 3 vols (1859) *£1.57½*
–Mill on the Floss 3 vols (1860 *£1.37½*
Mrs Gaskell Cranford (1858) *37½p*
Kingsley Westward Ho! (1855) 3 vols *£1.07½*
Tennyson Maud and other poems (1855) *25p*
Trollope The Warden (1855) *17½p*

FOOD ETC
FISH – oysters *3p per doz*
– sole *7p per pair*
GAME – duck *22p per pair*
– partridge *15p per brace*
– pheasant *14p each*

FURNISHINGS
BEDROOM
beds – 4ft 6ins iron bedstead *£1.95*
– 4ft 6ins japanned French bed *£1.35*
– oak 'shut-up' bed *£3.90*
– bolster and pillow *50p*
– 5ft quilt *90p*
DINING ROOM
– cabinets *£18*
– chair *£3*
– sideboard *£25*
DRAWING ROOM or LOUNGE
– couch *£10*

HEAT AND LIGHT
candles *4½p per lb*

HOUSING
Cost – back-to-back cottage *£150 - £200*
Rents – back-to back cottage *20p per week*
– London villa *£45 per annum*
– London lodging-house man *50p per week*
– a family *75p per week*

INCOME
boy under 11 *7p per week*
boy under 14 *10½p per week*
clerks junior *50p per week*
clerk *60p per week*
senior *£1.15 per week*
overlookers (cotton mills) *£1.70 per week*
semi-skilled (general) *85p per week*

SERVICES
SCHOOL FEES
City of London *£2.75 per term*
Harrow *Maximum £250 per annum*

TRANSPORT
London to Hampton Court *5p return*
London to Brighton *17½p return*

CLOTHING
flowered bonnet *42½p*
gored skirt *50p*

COST OF FIRST EDITIONS
Blackmore Lorna Doone (1869) 3 vols *£1.57½ (1871 edition 30p)*
Dickens Our mutual friend (1865) 2 vols *£1.10 (Octavo editions 1867 25p)*
George Eliot Silas Marner (1861) *60p*
W S Gilbert Bab Ballads (1868) *30p*
Kingsley Hereward the Wake (1866) 2 vols *£1.05*, 1 vol *30p*

FOOD etc
MEAT dried 'Chaqui' from America *1p per lb*

HOUSEHOLD
4-gallon water filter *£1.67½*

HOUSING
rent of two rooms *12½p per week*

INCOME
agricultural labourer *60p per week*
coachman *£2 per week*
gardener *£1.20 per week*

MISCELLANEOUS
da Vinci Mother and Child sold for *£209*
a Gainsborough portrait for £10,000

SERVICES
COVENT GARDEN THEATRE
– box *£2.10 to £6.30*
– stalls *£1.05*
– amphitheatre *12½p*
HAIRCUT man *2d (4/5p)*
– boy *1d (2/5p)*
SCHOOL FEES
City of London *£3 per term*

TRANSPORT
cabs *6d (2½p) per mile*, hire for a day *£1*
coach hire *£1.25 per day*

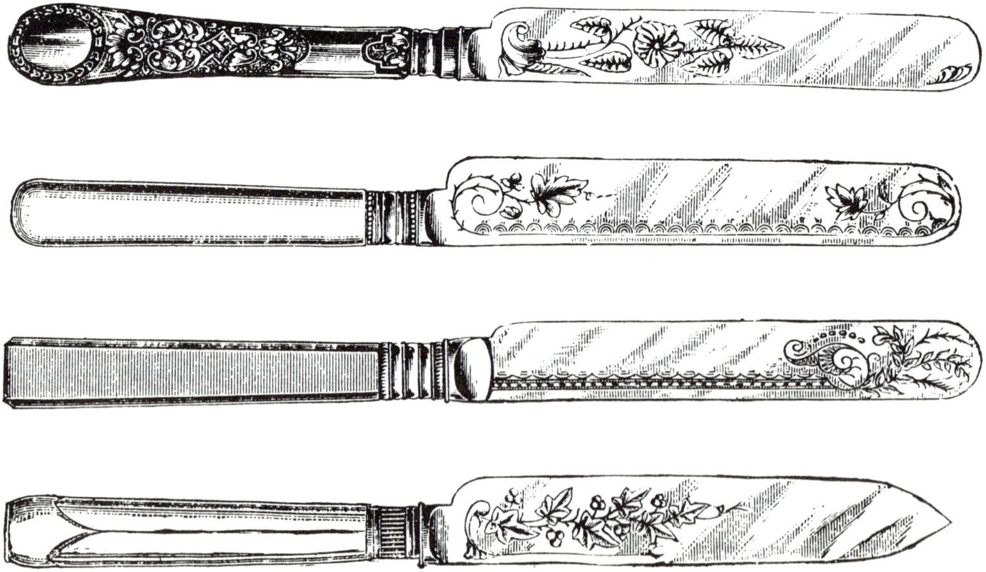

CLOTHING
dress materials – wide grosgrain *20p per yard*
– black silks *60p per yard*
kid gloves *10p per pair*
Ulster overcoat *£3.67*
seamen's shoes 1878 *67½p*

FOOD etc
FISH PRICES IN DETAIL
(London Market, 1877)
– bloater maximum *32½p per pad*
– cod *£6.80 per score*
– crabs *£1.50 per dozen*
– eels *4p per lb*
– kippers *21p per box*
– lobsters *£1.37 per dozen*
– mackerel *15p per dozen*
– mullet *37p per score*
– oysters – American *40p per 100*
oysters, common *40p per 100*
oysters, Dutch *43p per 100*
oysters, natives *95p per 100*
oysters, Spanish *25p per 100*
– salmon *25p per lb*
– sole *15p per pair*
– sprats *27p per bushel*
– whiting *67p per basket*
FRUIT DRIED
currants Vestizza *1½p per lb, best 2p per lb*
raisins Valencia *2p per lb*
MEAT
first cargo of frozen beef from the US retailed at *2p per lb*
tinned corned beef *1½p per lb*

FURNISHING AND EQUIPMENT
HOUSEHOLD
chairs, cane-seated *87½p for 6*
Windsor *£1.05 for 6*
curtains, muslin and lace *£1.25 per pair*
firelighters 500 for *52½p*
perambulators *£2*
refrigerators (ice-box) Duplex *£10.16*
tallow – Australian mutton *£2.17½ per cwt*
– rough fat *9½p per lb*
– town tallow *£2.21 per cwt*
water filter (charcoal) *£2*
GARDEN
bedding plants
– calceolaria *5p per doz*
– coleus *10p per doz*
– geranium *71p per doz* (bronze *10p per doz)*
– pelargonium *15p per doz*
– verbena *7½p per doz*
fruit trees, apple, pear and plum *7½p each*
currant bushes *10p each*
roses, standards *5p each,* half standards *4p each*

HEAT AND LIGHT
COAL PRICES
– Clay Cross *£1.30 per ton*
– Coke *80p per ton*
– Silkstone *£1.25 per ton*

HOUSING
RENTS 1875 Peabody Trust, one-room tenement *10p per week,* 2 rooms *17p,* 3 rooms *24p*

INCOME
agricultural labourer *65p per week*
foreman weaver *£2.25 per week*
silk worker *40p per week*
top manager *£1,000 per annum*

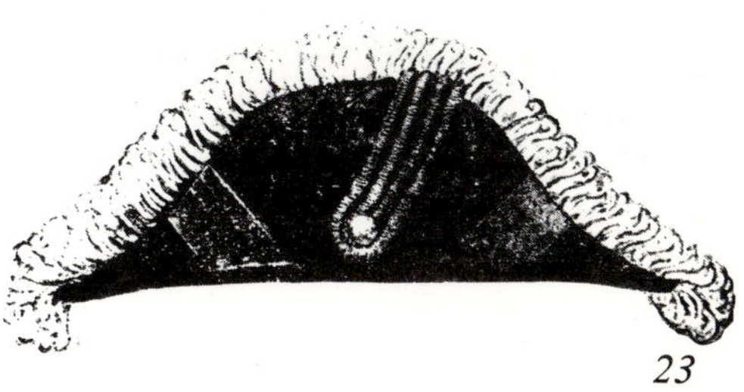

MISCELLANEOUS

FARM PRICES

– inferior meadow hay *£3.75*
– prime clover hay *£6 per load*
– prime meadow hay *£5.50*
– straw *£2.25 per load*

PERSONAL

pens 'They come as a boon and a blessing to men, The Pickwick, the Owl and the Waverley pen.' by post *5½p each*
pipes ADP briars, 'guaranteed against burning and cracking' from *5p each*
seamen's equipment (other items)
– comb *3p*
– knife *3½p*
– scissors *3p*
– scrubbing brush *2½p*
– towel *3p*
valentines from *1d (2/5p) upwards*

SERVICES

CLEANING

kid gloves *2d (4/5p) per pair*
black dyeing *2½p per pair*

DENTISTRY

Mr W S de Sax, Surgeon Dentist, Camden Road
'Enamelled teeth of surpassing beauty, lasting a lifetime, are perfect for eating and speaking, lifelike in appearance, can be worn on the most tender gums for years without removal.' Small tooth *12½p, sets £2*
EDUCATION Seymour School for Young Ladies, thoroughly good teaching, excellent references.
terms boarders with English and French inclusive *£30 per annum*

CLOTHING
LADIES
silk costume *£5.25*
corsets *25p per pair*
jackets, stockinette *£1*
mantles, silk *£2*
MEN
collars *2-3p each*
cuffs, detachable, *6p per pair*
fronts, detachable *6p each*
handkerchieves, coloured imitation silk *1½p each*
ties, fancy, *1½p each*
trousers *37p,* coloured tweed *45p* corduroy *22p*
BOYS
jerseys, navy *6p*
shirts *6p,* fancy wool *17½p*
trousers, cord *14p*
DRESS MATERIALS
cashmere, 45in French *12½p per yard*
crepe, silk *22½p per yard*
fabrics from *3p per yard*
flannel, scarlet and white cotton *3p per yard*
heavy wool *4½p per yard*
Melton cloths from *2½p per yard*
serge, all-wool 26in, summer *3p per yard*
shirtings, Oxford *1½p per yard*
suit lengths *£1.20 each*
tweeds, Scots dress from *3p per yard*
velveteen *7½p per yard*
FOOTWEAR
boots children's nailed, for school *12½p per pair*
men's side springs and balmorals *15p*
ladies *12p*
women's high-leg lace and button boots *15p*
for high-class wear, cycling boots *72p*
lace and elastic boots *64p*
shooting boots *92p*
repairs gents' sole and heel *16p* ladies *12p*

COST OF FIRST EDITIONS
Hardy The Mayor of Casterbridge (1886) 2 vols *£1.05 (new edition 1887-9 30p, 17½p and 10p)*
Shaw Widowers' Houses (1890) *12½p*
Tennyson Locksley Hall (1886) *30p*

FOOD etc
baking powder, digestive egg *8½p per lb*
biscuits, Garibaldi, gingernuts and lemon drops *1½p per lb*
carbonate of soda *1½p per lb*
cigars *1p each*
fruit dried apple rings *2½p per lb*
– currants, figs *1p per lb*
– muscatels *4p per lb*
– prunes, raisins, sultanas *1½p per lb*
– fresh lemons 26 for *5p*
– oranges; fine St. Michael 40 for *5p*
– fine large 30 for *5p*
– ordinary 50 for *5p*
jam greengage *2p per lb*
– marmalade *2p per lb*
– raspberry *6p per lb*
lard *2p per lb*
lentils, split *2½p per lb*
meat beef, back ribs *3p per lb*
brisket *3p,* flanks *3p*
mutton and lamb breast *1½p*
shoulder, neck and forequarters *2½p per lb*
pork loin and neck *3½p* hands *3p* heads *2½p*

nuts almonds, Barcelona, Brazil and
– Spanish *1½p per quart*
– bitter almonds *6p per quart*
– Jordan almonds *7½p per quart*
– sweet almonds *5p per quart*
– best coconuts *1p each*
oatmeal, Scots 7lb for *5p*
onions, Spanish 8lb for *2½p*
peas, dried *1p per quart*
pickles, pint bottle *2¼p*, gallon jar *15p*
rice 10lb for *5p*
sago *1p per lb*
semolina *2½p per lb*
Swiss milk *2¼p per lb*
Nestle's *2¾p per lb*
tapioca *4p per lb*
treacle, golden syrup 7lb for *5p*

FURNISHINGS

BEDROOM
double feather bed with pillows *£2*
– iron bedstead *62½p*
DINING ROOM
suite comprising 11 articles, solid mahogany *£14.25*
DRAWING ROOM
suite comprising 15 articles, walnut *£6.87½*

HEATING AND LIGHTING

candles, wax *2¼p per lb*
stoves – Bruce oil *77½p*
– American 'burns anything' with boiler *£5.90*

HOUSEHOLD

CROCKERY
– dinner set, 50 pieces *82½p*
– jugs, set of 3 *5p*
– quart decanter, cut glass *12½p*
– tea set *50p*
– toilet set *11½p*
– trinket set *11½p*
– tumbler *½p*
– wineglasses *½p each*, claret glass *1½p*, hock glasses *2½p*

FABRICS
– baize, oiled for table use *2½p per yard*
– calico, white and grey *1p per yard*
– cretonnes *1p per yard*
reversible *2p per yard*
– damask, red *2½p per yard*
– glass cloth, check *1p per yard*
– prints, fast colours *1p per yard*
– sheeting, white 70 ins wide *2½p per yard*
– tapestry from *7p per yard*
– towelling (roller) *1p per yard*
FLOOR COVERINGS
carpet, Brussels from *10p per yard*
– Kidderminster from *7½p*
– felt squares *25p each* (size not given)
floor cloths, 18in *1p per yard*
– 36in *2¾p per yard* (Note: This kind of cloth, smooth-faced with stout canvas backing was used before linoleum came into use)
hearthrugs from *7½p*
stair carpet 18in *1½p per yard*
– 32 in *2p per yard*
– 45 in *3p per yard*
– 54in *4p per yard* (quality not stated)
mangles *£2*, portable *£3*, wringers *£1*
perambulators – bassinettes, Harris Victoria from *£1.50*
superior *£2.50*
soap, carbolic *1p per lb*
– cold water soap *1½p*
– yellow *1¼p*
– Hudson's washing powder *2½p per lb*
starch *3p per lb*
towels, honeycomb and Turkish *2p each*
washing machine, steam *£3.15*

THE GARDEN

BULBS

– anemone *5p per 100*
– crocus *7½p per 100*
– daffodils, *2½p per dozen*
– hyacinth *10p per dozen*
– jonquils, narcissus, tulips *4p per dozen*
– ranunculus *2½p per dozen*
– snowdrop *12½p per 100*

SEEDS

– broad beans *2½p per quart*
– cabbage and savoy *2½p per oz*
– parsnip *1¼p per oz*
– peas *3½p per quart*
– scarlet runners *5p per quart*
– turnip *¾p per oz*

PERSONAL

– bathchair *£1.40*
– knitting pattern, paper *5p*
– pens, fountain and 'stylo' *12½p*
– reading lamp, gas *£1.05*
– talking machine, Anglophone disc, with records *£1.07*
– umbrella, silk *12½p*
– watch, silver case *65p*

SERVICES

CLEANING

feathers cleaned, curled and dyed from *2½p each*
gloves from *1p per pair*

TRANSPORT (private)

Brougham *£175*, with horse *£225*

CLOTHING
LADIES
camisoles *15p*
chemises *35p*
combinations *28p*
fleecy kneecaps *14p per pair*
knickers *13p per pair*
nightdresses *30p*
skirts, long cloth *50p*
MEN
gloves, French calf *14p per pair*
handkerchieves, Irish linen *40p per dozen*
hats, soft felt *37½p*
hat case, leather, bucket-shaped *75p*
neckwear, collars, linen *32p per dozen*
–cuffs, detachable 4¾in deep *5p per pair*
–fronts, detachable *4p each*
shirts *6½p* dress shirts *15p*
trousers *37p*
undervests *20p*

COST OF FIRST EDITIONS
Conrad Almayer's folly (1895) *30p*
– The nigger of the Narcissus (1897) *30p*
Kipling The jungle book (1894) *30p*
Webb, Sidney and Beatrice A history of trade unionism (1894) *90p*
Wells The stolen bacillus *30p*
– The invisible man *17½p*

FOOD etc
almonds Jordan *10p per lb*
bananas *1d* (less than ½p each)
biscuits – gingernuts and petit beurre *2½p per lb*
– marie *3p per lb*
– tea biscuits *1½p per lb*
Bovril *8p per 4oz bottle*
cake, cherry Dundee *4p per lb*
chocolate creams *6p per lb*
chocolate eclairs 8 for *5p*
cocoa *12½p per lb*
cream of Tartar *5p per lb*
eucalyptus lozenges *15p per lb*
glycerine *15p per quart*
FISH – halibut *3p per lb*
– herrings 6 for *1½p*
– Whitstable oysters, at table *17½p per dozen*
hampers for school, containing:
2lb currant cake, 1 ham and chicken sausage, 1 jar potted meat, 1 jar jam, 1 jar marmalade, 1 bottle sweets, 12 oranges, 2lb mixed nuts *25p*

1lb tea, 1 turkey (or a 7lb joint of prime beef), 1 bottle port (or 24 oranges and 2lb mixed nuts), 2lb Brittany butter and 1lb sausages *52½p*

2lb tea, 36 oranges, 2lb mixed nuts, 2lb plum pudding, 1 ham, 1 turkey (or a 7lb joint of prime beef), 1lb Brittany butter and 1lb sausages *£1.05½*
hams, whole York *7½p per lb*
hops *12½p per lb*
ice cream, vanilla *17½p per quart*
Irish moss *4p per lb*
lard *3p per lb*
linseed 7lb for *7½p*
liqueurs – Creme de Menthe *22½p per bottle* (quantity not stated)
liquorice root *18p per lb*
liquors – porter *5p per pint*
– stout *7p per pint*
spirits – brandy *23p per bottle*
– gin *11p per bottle*
– rum *18p per bottle*
– whisky *17p per bottle*
wines – Beaujolais *90p per dozen bottles*
–champagne, Moet and Chandon white dry *£3 per dozen*
– claret, Bordeaux *52½p per dozen*
oats, crushed *2½p per 2lb packet*
oil, Batty's frying *14p per gallon*
orange *1d* (less than ½p)
peppermint lozenges *10p per jar*
prunes *1½p per lb*

GENTLEMEN'S HOSIERY, &c.

No. 18 DEPARTMENT.—*FIRST FLOOR.*

PYJAMA SLEEPING SUITS.

Pyjama Sleeping Suits .. .. 5/6, 8/11, 13/6 and 14/6

Carriage Paid on all parcels over £1 in value, subject to certain limitations mentioned on page 4,

PURE WATER.

THE WAY TO OBTAIN IT IS TO USE A

SILICATED CARBON FILTER.

It will remove Germs and Impurities of all kinds.

IMPORTANT.—The prices have been revised, and are for a *special* manufacture of Filters, the object being to place before our customers a thorough genuine article in preference to a cheap and worthless one.

REFRIGERATOR FILTER,

With Patent Self-Aërating Cover and Movable Block. Made in Porous Terra-cotta Ware, which acts with remarkable power as a cooler, and renders this Filter invaluable, especially in Tropical Climates, affording a Cool Draught of Pure Water. Capacity, Two Gallons. Price, with Silver-plated Tap, 31/6. Extra charges of Granular Silicated Carbon, 1/6 each. Specially adapted for Tropical Climates.

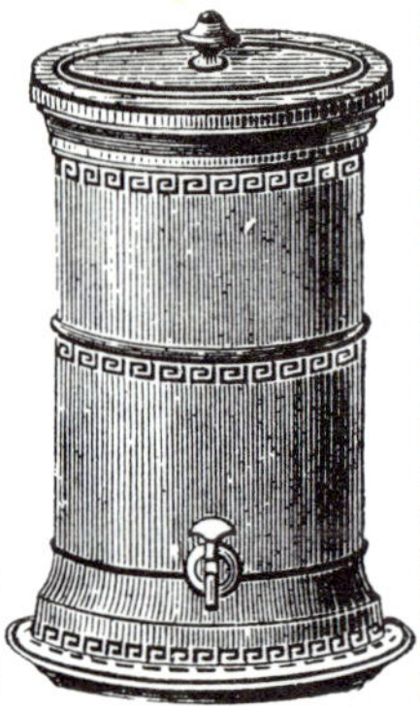

TRIPLE FILTRATION.

PRIZE FILTER,

With Patent Self-Aerating Cover and Movable Block. An Etruscan Vase, having inside it a movable pan, into which the Silicated Carbon filtering medium is fitted. It is made of Porous Ware, which acts with remarkable power as a Refrigerator, keeping the water deliciously cool. Capacity, about Two Gallons. Price, with Silver-plated Tap, 70/0. Extra charges of Granular Silicated Carbon, 2/0 each.

The granular Silicated Carbon is not shown in the drawing for the sake of clearness.

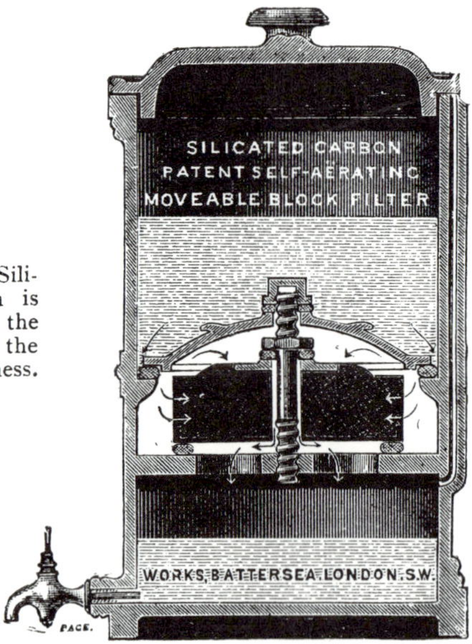

Extra charges of Silicated Carbon for surrounding the movable blocks. Prices per charge, ½ gal. 0/6½, 1 gal. 0/9½ 2 gal. 1/3, 4 gal. 1/9½.

SELF-AERATING FILTER.

The solid block is surrounded with granular carbon (recommended). ½ gal., 11/6; 1 gal., 13/6; 2 gal., 18/6; 4 gal., 29/6; 6 gal., 35/6; 8 gal., 47/6; 12 gal., 65/0.

For the 1890s goat-cart owner a complete harness cost £2.00

sardines 18oz tin *3p*
sulphur, flowers of *1½d per lb* (slightly more than ½p)
treacle *1p per ib*

FOOTWEAR
good quality boots *55p*
light boots *35p*
nailed boots *90p*
tan boots *40p*
gents' walking shoes *70p*
ladies' walking shoes *60p* (extra good *£1.40*)

FURNISHINGS
BEDROOM
blankets, York *30p pair*
chairs *37p each*
quilt, down, double *£1.50*
sheeting, cotton, double width *6½p per yard*
suite, complete *£18.00*
DINING ROOM AND LOUNGE
carpeting, Axminster 27in wide *25p per yard*
– tapestry carpeting *15p per yard*
floor covering, oilcloth *15p per yard*
suite, complete *£30.50*

HEATING AND LIGHTING
gas fire with asbestos radiants *£1.25*
kitchen nuts *90p per ton*
sperm candles (cheap variety) 3lb for *25p*

HOUSEHOLD
ammonia *4p per pint*
bath, Oxford hip 44in *£1.07*
blacking *2p per dozen cakes*
black lead *2½p per lb*
carbonate of soda, household 7lb *6p*
carpet sweeper, Grand Rapids *52½p*
castor oil, 16oz *4½p*
chair, cheap quality folding, pitch pine splines *15p*
chip basket for garden 17½x9½in *5p*
cod liver oil *42½p per pint*
cold frame for garden, red deal 4x6ft *£1.80*
dustbin, round 18x24in high *41p*
gum tragacanth *20p per lb*
kennel, portable wooden 3x1¾x3ft high *£1.32*
kettle, wrought iron country, 4 pint *13p*
matches *3½p per dozen boxes*

pan, copper omelette 8in *20p*
perambulator with canopy *£3.00*
refrigerator (ice-box) wooden, zinc-lined, painted and grained 3¼x2 ft *£5.54*
sewing machine, Wellington hand *£2.50* with cover, treadle Frister and Rossman with cover *£7.00*
household steps with seven treads *28p*
summerhouse, lean-to, 10x6ft tall *£11.00*
– floor extra *£1.50*
towel roller with brackets *5p*
watering-can with short spout, 2 gals *11½p*
wheelbarrow, elm and ash, 32x22in at top *£1.64*
wringer, clothes, Iron Tudor stand machine with wooden rollers *£2.80*

HOUSING

two-bedroomed cottage *£190.00*
four-bedroomed house *£650.00*
rents, house, working-class *35p per week*
– tenements, one-room *14p*
– two-rooms *23p*
– three-rooms *30p*

INCOME

agricultural labourer *90p per week*
butler *£100 per annum*
footman, upper *£50.00 per annum*

The Victorian watchholder with night-light, complete for 11p

cook housekeeper *£80.00 per annum*
governess *£75.00 per annum*
head housemaid *£30.00 per annum*
miner *£1.75 per week*
nanny *£40.00 per annum*
skilled worker (general) *£1.90 per week*

PERSONAL

belts, cholera belts *14p*
pregnancy belts *35p*
cascara pills *11½p per 100*
alarm clocks, one-day *22p*
cufflinks, 9 carat gold, ornamental *90p*
Facial 'BEARDS! BEARDS! BEARDS! Volosci, the only hair-growing specific, *1s (5p) or 2s.6d (12½p)* for three boxes'
MOUSTACHES 'Why is one young man able to grow a luxuriant moustache at 18 and even younger and another can't show any hair on his face at perhaps 26? GRENADIER, the hair-root stimulant *1s (5p) a box, three boxes 2s.6d (12½p)* post free. Despatched in plain cover'
fountain pens, Swan *52½p*
moustache cup and saucer *25p*
notepaper, cream laid 7x4 7/8in *7p per ream*
sal volatile *19p per pint*
soap, John Knight's 3lb bar *3p*, one 7lb box family toilet soap *13p*
spectacles and eyeglasses, light gold-framed spectacles, best pebbles *90p*
– pince-nez, gold frame, spring grip *90p*
– steel spectacles *12½p*
– spectacles with curled sides for riding *15p*
hygienic towelettes, *4p per dozen*
Vaseline *6p per lb*
watches, English lever open-face *£3.15*
– good keyless *£10*
– schoolboy's *60p*

SERVICES

SCHOOL FEES

Eton 1896 *£8.40* per term plus house payment of *£110.00* per annum
City of London School *£5.25* per term

footwear repairs, soling and heeling with rivets, gents *17½p,* ladies *11p*
soling and heeling with hand sewing, gents *20p,* ladies *14p*

SPORTS AND PASTIMES

camera, Kodak cheap *£1.00* Kodak regular 3¼x4¼in *£8.37*
cricket bats *64p*
flutes, Boehm *£7.50*
footballs *35p*
golf clubs *30p*, balls *50p per dozen*
paints, artists' in 2in tubes; oil *4p each,* water colour in 2in tubes or cakes *5p each*
pianos, Bechstein grand 8ft *£210.00*
– upright concert grand 4ft 5½in high *£105.00*
roller skates, ordinary *35p*, ball-bearing extension *£1.27*
tennis balls *40p per dozen,* racquets *50p*
trunks for travelling, compressed cane 36x18in *£3.14*, japanned 30in *67½p*
violins, superior French *£2.50*
Violoncellos, copies of Italian masters *£4.00*

Cost of this 1895 stove fitted with four burners was £2.12½

'Handsome mahogany Half-Tester bedstead' was the 1890s description of this handsome piece of bedroom furniture. Price £19

COST OF FIRST EDITIONS
Wells A modern Utopia (1905) *37½p*
Kipps (1905) *30p*

FOOD etc
almonds *2p per lb*
butter beans *1½p per lb*
biscuits – cream crackers *2p per lb*
– digestive *1¼p per lb*
– garibaldi *2½p per lb*
– lemon cream *3p per lb*
– macaroons *7½p per lb*
Bovril 4oz for *9p*
cider *70p per dozen bottles*
cocoa *8p per lb*

FISH – bloaters from *26p per dozen*
– cod *1½p per lb*
– haddock – finnan *3p per dozen*
– plaice *1½p per lb*
flour *4p per 7lb*
gelatine *6p per lb*
ginger wine *57½p per dozen bottles*
ham, thick back *4p per lb*
– York *4½p per lb*
honey *5p per lb*
jams and marmalade *2½p per lb*
lentils, split *¾p per lb,* whole German *2p per lb*
macaroni *1½p per lb*
Marmite 2oz jar *3p*
meat, Australian corned beef *5½p per lb*
mustard *4p per lb*
oatmeal, Scots coarse *½p per lb*
peas, split *4p per 7lb*
pepper, white-grained *7½p per lb*
raisins – muscatel 14lb for *43p*
– sultana 14lb for *34p*
– Valencia 14lb for *28p*
salt, household 7lb for *1½p*
semolina 7lb for *5½p*
sugar – caster 7lb for *7p*
– granulated 7lb for *7p*
– icing *2p per lb*
sweets – acid drops *2p per lb*
– barley sugar *3p per lb*
– chocolate, plain *6p per lb*
– chocolate, almonds *11p per lb*
– chocolate creams *11p per lb*
– chocolate peppermint creams *9p per lb*
– nougat *14p per lb*
– peppermint bullseyes *3p per lb*
peppermint rock *4p per lb*
tea – China *15p per lb*
– best Indian *11p per lb*
treacle – Golden Syrup 2lb for *2½p*
– West Indian 2lb for *2½p*
vermicelli 4lb for *6p*
vinegar *4p per quart*
wines – champagne *£4.90 per dozen bottles*
– claret *£2.50 per dozen*
– port *£1.70 per dozen*
– sherry *£2.10 per dozen*

FURNISHINGS
BEDROOM
chest of drawers *85p*
plain servant's bed, woollen mattress *£1.75*

HEATING AND LIGHTING
candles *4p per lb box*
firelighters 250 for *33p*
firewood bundles 100 for *17½p*
matches, safety *3¾p per dozen boxes*
– non-safety *2p per dozen*

HOUSEHOLD
bath bricks 12 for *5p*
blacking for shoes *49p per dozen bottles*
boot polish, 4 tins for *7½p*
soaps, toilet, box of 3 tablets *5p*
silver – dessert spoons *£3.85 per dozen*
– table spoons *£5.70 per dozen*
– teaspoons *£1.90 per dozen*
toilet services including ewer, basin, soapdish, brush holder, chamber and soap bowl, single *£1.25*, double *£2*

HOUSING

RENTS cottages *£18 per annum*
double-fronted house *£42 per annum*
Board-residence *£1.05 per week*

INCOME

clerk (railway) *£1.50 per week*
foreman (general) *£2.25 per week*
miner *£1.75 per week*
London turner *£2 per week*

SERVICES

DENTISTRY, extractions *5p*
false teeth (dentures) *£1.05 per set*
single teeth *12½p each*
SCHOOL FEES
Eton *£10.50 per term plus £115 per annum*

Tartan silk ladies blouse. Cost £1.29

1911–14

CLOTHING

DRESS MATERIALS
– cambric, striped, 32in wide *12p per yd*
– coatings and suitings *£1 per yd*
– flannel, cream 27 in wide *15p per yd*
– gabardine suiting for sportswear 28 in wide *22½p per yd*
– georgette 40 in wide *27½p per yd*
– gingham 31 in wide *12p per yd*
– Viyella 31 in wide *24½p per yd*
– voile, printed 40 in wide *15p per yard*
FOOTWEAR
– quilted slipper boots *12½p per pair*
– shoes, court *52½p per pair*
– patent dress *50p per pair*
'Jackson's boots and hats are fine, ten and six *(52½p)* and three and nine *(18¾p)*' (newspaper advertisement)
HIGH-CLASS LADIES' WEAR
– blouses *£1.50*
– combinations *£1.50*
– coney seal coat *£78.75*
– corsets *£1,* 'Fitu' corsets *7p,* special *20p*
– frock, jersey cloth *£4.50*
– gloves 75p
– shirts *£1.50*
– sleeping suits *£1*
– tailored suit *£8*
– underskirt *£1.50*

COST OF FIRST EDITIONS

Shaw Androcles and the lion (1912) *30p*
Wells The world set free (1914) *30p*
The wife of Sir Isaac Harman (1914) *30p*

FOOD etc

cigars, Havana Enricos finos *£3 per 100,* la Corona Corona *£5.50 per 100*
meat, beef, chilled *3p per lb*
lamb breast *4p per lb,* loin *2½p per lb*

PHOTOGRAPHIC APPARATUS—*continued.*

FLASH LAMPS.

The "TODD TORRETT" MAGNESIUM LAMP.

The special features of this Lamp are:—The production at will of an INSTANTANEOUS or CONTINUOUS Flash; complete combustion of the powder; flash in form of large sheet, thus affording a large illuminating surface.

Price, complete in box, 12/6.

SQUEEGEEING SHEETS.

Xylonite Sheets, one side matt and one side polished surface,
7 by 5, 0/6; 9 by 7, 1/0; 11 by 9, 1/6 each.

All the above are delivered Carriage Free subject to the Conditions set forth on page 4.

No. 3.—Chain-Stitch Machine, with accessories... ... ... £1 12 0
Stand and table for ditto £1 2 6 Polished box ... 0 7 6

No. 4.—Automatic Hand Machine, Chain-Stitch, with accessories £2 12 6
Stand and table for ditto ... £1 2 6 Polished pine case for travelling 0 7 6

FURNISHINGS
carpeting, Axminster *30p per yd*
oilcloth *18p per yd*

HOUSEHOLD
carpet sweeper, Grand Rapids ball-bearing *75p*
clocks, repeater alarm *31¼p, 400-*day, glass case, brass base 11in high *92½p,* with ball pendulum *£1.05*
reading lamp, Cambridge telescopic candle (reflector) *37½p*
tool cabinet, pine 21x14 in with 26 tools and screws, *£1.97½,* in oak *£2.37½*
typewriters, Oliver (rebuilt) *£13.50,* Remington (rebuilt) *£10.50*

HOUSING
1914, semi-detached house, London *£600, provinces £450.*

INCOME
bricklayer *£2.06 per week*
clerks, bank *£2.80 per week,* civil service *£116 per annum,* business *£96 per annum*
managers *£250 per annum*

No. 74.

No. 74.—Height 5 in., Dial 2 in. Polished Brass Frame. 1-day Lever Timepiece, 9/9.

village schoolmaster *£200 per annum*

PERSONAL
books for children, Herbert Strang's Annual, cloth *25p,* picture boards *17½p,* Chatterbox Annual cloth *19p,* picture boards *17½p,* diaries Letts Schoolboy's Art linen *5p* leather *10p,* Scout's khaki cloth *2½p* leather *5p*
transformations from human hair, curl cluster *£2.10,* front transformation *£9.45,* tails of hair 18 in *£1.25,* 22 in *£2.10,* 28 in £4.50
umbrellas *£1* each
walking sticks *25p each*
watches, Enigma *25p each,* 9-day silver *£2.37½,* dress watch, 18 carat *£7.50,* wrist watch, sterling silver with strap *87½p*

SPORTS AND PASTIMES
billiard tables 10x5ft wide with balls, cue rack and accessories *£37,* full size table *£63*
cameras, Brownie *82½p,* Kodak folding pocket *£4.50,* vest-pocket *£1.50*
cinematograph *£8*
cornet *£1.50*
doll, 18½ in high, dressed *34½p*
euphonium *£2.37½*
fiddlephone (Japanese fiddle) *77½p*
football *50p*
golf balls *90 per dozen,* clubs *25p each*
gramophones, cabinet disc machine *£7.50* cylinder 17½p
cylinder with flower horn, camel hair chip brush, winding crank and oak carrying case *£4.75*
disc – 'runs for 5 minutes at a wind' *£2.19*
gramophone trumpet basket for carrying horn 31 in *37½p*
hornless, with wooden doors to soundbox *£3.75*
junior disc with flower horn, 'can be wound up while play-

ing' with 200 needles *£5.50*
magic lantern, good quality *£2.50*
models, biplane, Sopwith tractor *£1.05,*
locomotives, Great Western Passenger Express, steam, heated by spirit lamp *£1.62½*
London and North Western, Queen Mary, clockwork *75p*
doll's mansion 18x18½ in, 4 rooms and furniture *59p*
motor bus, clockwork *14½p*
soldiers, box containing 83 foot and mounted toy soldiers *4½p*
station, scale model with stationmaster, passengers, guards etc and moveable barriers *92½p*
steam engine, vertical, with oxidised brass boiler and whistle *12½p*
motor cycling 1911 Triumph 3½hp roadster *£48.75,* TT racer £50, spark plug *17½p,* bulb horn *42½p*
organ, Angelus harmonium *£7.87½*
outfits, cowboy, best quality *67½p*
American Indian, best quality *87½p*
pianos, Ideal player piano *£47.25,* cottage piano *£15.75*
playing cards *5p per pack*
rocking horse, old style 3ft 3ins high with 6ft 6ins rocker and furniture *£1.87½*
roller skates *23p per pair.* The best, with aluminium wheels *£1.75 per pair*
top, gyroscopic hopping *2½p*
violins, reproductions of old masters, Stradivarius *£8.40,* Guarnerius *£10.50*
violoncellos *£5.57½*
wireless telegraphic set, complete (from Benetfink of Cheapside) *£1.97½*

The spring mattress of the early twenties

1915 - 1970

One of the results of a major war is an increase in prices. The entry of Great Britain into the war in August 1914 caused the cost of living to increase immediately by one-seventh. Later in the war years, food shortages and the great demand for war materials caused another upsurge of prices so that by 1920 the old pre-1914 wage-and-price structure had altered considerably.

The immediate post-war period was one of intense disappointment. People had hoped for prosperity but instead, trade was depressed, unemployment was high, wages were low and prices fell correspondingly. It was not so bad for those who were in work, for they were on the whole able to maintain their standard of living. The greatest sufferers were again the unemployed and certain public servants whose pay was reduced in an economy drive. There was unrest in all the major industries – iron, coal, textiles and agriculture.

In 1923 the Government considered that the economy had become more stable, and in an effort to boost trade with the Empire and Commonwealth a great British Empire Exhibition was organised at Wembley. But between this date and 1933, Great Britain went through two serious crises. The first came after 1925, the year in which Winston Churchill, who was at that time Chancellor of the Exchequer, put British currency back on the gold standard. It is now generally acknowledged that this was a mistake, for it over-valued the pound making it worth more in foreign countries, thereby raising the prices of British goods to the foreigner, though imports into Britain became cheaper. The move was unfortunate at a time when home industries were already suffering badly. In 1926 the dissatisfaction of the British worker showed itself in the General Strike which collapsed after nine days.

The second crisis came after the great Wall Street crash of 1929 in the United States. This brought about the failure of innumerable business concerns in Great Britain and everywhere else in Europe. In 1931 the gold standard had to be abandoned. In another great economy drive salaries, especially those of men and women in public service, were again cut. By 1932 the unemployment figures had risen to almost three million. With the dole reduced from 17 shillings (85p) a week to 15/3d (76p) for men, the suffering of this unfortunate section of the community can hardly be imagined in our day.

After the abandonment of the gold standard the value of the pound began to decline abroad and the cost of home-produced goods went down. After 1933 trade and industry gradually picked up and prices started to rise slowly. For all but the unemployed who still numbered more than a million, the standard of living was either maintained or improved. The middle classes in particular enjoyed something of a brief spell of comparative prosperity. Modern fixtures and appliances in the home such as refrigerators, electric fires, hair dryers, cookers and sewing machines became more common; radio had by this time penetrated almost every household, a start had already been made with the development of television and more families were able to buy cars.

Then came the war of 1939-45. By this time the lessons of previous decades had been learnt. With price controls and rationing the Government succeeded in keeping down the cost of living in terms of money to no more than one-third above the 1939 level. Between 1914 and 1919 it had been 100 per cent.

The peace of 1945 brought a flood of demands for all manner of goods from all parts of the world. Countries that had been at war needed to rebuild their shattered towns, to re-establish their industries, and in addition to these, the now familiar third world – countries just beginning to develop and attached neither to the communist world nor the west – was emerging into independence and these peoples, too, were in the market for goods and machinery.

For some years Britain went through a period of austerity accompanied by sacrifice and rationing, but with full employment. The rise in prices which followed the end of the war continued throughout the fifties and sixties, but in spite of pay pauses, pay freezes, restraint, a prices and incomes board and early warning systems to give notice of possible economic trouble, the working man was at least as well off as before, for wages had increased in rough proportion to the cost of living. At one time a famous British prime minister was able to tell the public that they had never had it so good.

By 1964 retail prices were double what they had been in 1945, and by the late sixties it was realised that something had to be done to correct the imbalance. Though prices had begun to rise at a more rapid rate, economic growth was for some reason slowing down, and the country as a whole was spending more than its people were earning. In November 1967 the Government were forced to devalue the pound in the hope of stimulating exports and discouraging imports. In spite of reassurances that money would not be worth less in the family man's wage packet, the pound diminished in value during the first year by 5½ per cent, and in the second by nearly the same figure.

This was the beginning of a price spiral that was to present governments, trade unions, employers' associations and the public at large with the one great problem of the seventies – how to conquer the bogy of inflation.

This part of the book shows some price changes occurring again and again within a single ten-year period. In the case of two (petrol and cigarettes) the figures have been averaged and the number of changes given. In certain important cases such as postages, newspapers, railway fares and TV licences, every change has been recorded, and the same applies to state retirement pensions. There were also some sudden and frequent price rises during the first world war and these too have been given in detail.

SERVANTS' CAPS AND APRONS.

A.D.G. 501

White Lawn Apron, in a very good quality, trimmed scalloped edging .. 2/6

Coronet Cap to match, trimmed black velvet.. .. .. 1/6

Collar and Cuffs to match 1/11½

A.D.G. 506

Plain Apron, with round or square bibs, and large pockets 2/11, 3/6, 4/11

Sister Dora Cap, plain
In White Muslin 1/1
In White Linen 2/1

A.D.G. 503

Plain White Muslin Apron, with wide double hem .. 2/11

Coronet Cap to match, finished black velvet 1/8

Collar and Cuffs to match, the set 1/6

A.D.G. 504

White Check Muslin Tea Apron, trimmed lace .. 1/11½

Cap to match, finished black velvet 1/6

Collar and Cuffs to match, the set 1/7

A.D.G. 501

A.D.G. 502

A.D.G. 503

A.D.G. 504

A.D.G. 505

A.D.G. 506

A.D.G. 507

A.D.G. 502

Beige or White Organdi Apron, trimmed lace 4/6

Coronet Cap to match, trimmed black velvet 1/11½

Collar and Cuffs to match, the set 2/6

A.D.G. 505

Afternoon Apron, trimmed embroidery 2/11

Sister Dora Cap, with elastic at back, trimmed veining 1/5

A.D.G. 500

Afternoon Apron, of good quality Lawn, trimmed embroidery 4/3

Cap with Embroidered Front, trimmed black velvet 1/11½

A.D.G. 507

White Spotted Muslin Apron, with plain hem .. 2/11

Cap to match, with elastic at back for short hair 2/6

Collar and Cuffs to match 1/11

ALL PRICES ARE SUBJECT TO MARKET FLUCTUATIONS.

FOOD DRINK TOBACCO	1915 – 20	1921 – 30
Bacon per lb	Streaky 13p 1920	Streaky 7p
Bread 4lb	1915 3½p 1920 5p	1930 3½p
Butter per lb	13p	10p
Cabbage per lb	½p	½p
Cheese per lb	7p	7p
Coffee per quarter	6½p	6½p
Eggs per doz	1915 10p 1919-20 17½p	11p
Lard per lb	7p	5p
Beer per pint	1918 2½p	2½p
Whisky per bottle	62½p	75p
Margarine per lb	5½p	3½p
Meat Beef per lb	ribs 9p	5p
Pork	4p	4p
Sirloin	10p	7p
Potatoes per 7lb	1916 3p 1920 5½p	5½p
Sugar per lb	1915-19 3p 1920 5½p	2½p
Tea per lb	14p	11½p
Tobacco cigarettes	Players' Medium 20 4½p (5 advances)	5p
Tobacco pipe per oz	5p	5p

CLOTHING	1915 – 20	1921 – 30
Men's overcoat	£2.50	£3.50
Shirt	£1	60p
Shoes	£1.05	£1.50
Suit	£3	£3.50
Women's coats	£3.50	£5.25

1931 – 40	1941 – 44	1945 – 50	1951 – 60	1961 – 70
5p	7p	8½p	Smoked 15p Streaky 12p	26p 21p
4p	4p	5p	10½p	16p
6p	1942 5p	6½p	10p	20p
½p	1p	3p	3½p	4p
4½p	5½p	5p	12½p	17p
8p	10p	10p	15p	18p (instant)
7½p	10½p	12½p	23p	37p
1931 2½p	1942 4p	1945 5p	6p	13p
3p	5p	6½p	6p	6p
65p	£1.10	1950 £1.70	£1.80	£2.42½
2½p	3p	3½p	5p	10p
4½p	5½p	Brisket 7p	8p	14p
5p	5p	leg 7½p belly 7p	leg 10p belly 12p	leg 15p belly 16p
6p	7½p	9p	16p	32p
5½p	6p	7p	12p	1962-9 1½p per lb 1970 2½p per lb
1p	1942 1½p	1947 1p	1p	3p
12p	22p	26p	36p	36p
6p (6 advances)	11p (2 advances)	16p (2 advances)	22p (5 advances)	29p (9 advances)
5p	5p (very scarce)	5p	15p	20p

1931 – 40	1941 – 44	1945 – 50	1951 – 60	1961 – 70
£4.50	£6.50	£10	£12	£14
60p	£1	£1.50	£1.75	£2
£3	£3.50	£4.50	£5.25	£6
£4	£6	£7.50	£12	£14
£6	£6.75	£7.50	£10.50	£15

CLOTHING	1915 – 20	1921 – 30
Shoes	£1	£1
Stockings	17p	20p

FURNISHING	1915 – 20	1921 – 30
Bedroom, bed with mattress	£15	£20
Blankets (double)	£1.75	£1.75
Sheets (double)	£1.25	£1.30
Dining room table	£12	£12
Lounge carpeting (Axminster)	70p per sq yd (when available)	70p
Electric blanket	non-existent	developing slowly
Cooker (gas or electric)	TRADE DEVELOPING SLOWLY	
Fire (gas or electric)		
Refrigerator		
Radio	TRADE BEGINNING	Crystal set £2 3 valve set 1927 £20
Sewing machine (electric)	TRADE DEVELOPING	
Television	NON-EXISTENT	
Vacuum Cleaner (electric)	No models	£10

HEAT & LIGHT	1915 – 20	1921 – 30
Coal (per ton)	£1.35	£1.50
Electricity (lighting per unit)	3½d (1 2/5p)	4½d (1 4/5p)
Gas (per therm)	4p (5p in 1920)	3½p

SERVICES	1915 – 20	1921 – 30
Postage (inland letter)	1915 1d (2/5p) to 1oz 1920 2d (4/5p) to 3oz	1922 1½d (3/5p) to 3oz

1931 – 40	1941 – 44	1945 – 50	1951 – 60	1961 – 70
£1	£1.25	£1.50	£3	£4.50
20p	15p	15p	20p	25p

1931 – 40	1941 – 44	1945 – 50	1951 – 60	1961 – 70
£20	£20	£30	£35	£40
£1.50	£2	£3	£4	£5
£1.40	£2	£2.50	£2.75	£3
£15	£15	£18	£20	£20
70p	90p	£1.40	£1.50	£2
		£10	1957 £11	low voltage £12
£7		£12	£23	£50
£2.50	WAR CONDITIONS. NEW ELECTRIC GOODS ETC. OFF THE MARKET	£6	£15	£20
£50		£50	£50	£60
£20		£25	£30	Stereo £90
£20		£35	£40	£60
Trade commencing		£80	£90	£90
standard £19		£30	£35	£40

1931 – 40	1941 – 44	1945 – 50	1951 – 60	1961 – 70
£1.35	£1.70	£3.60	£7.66	£15
3d (1 1/5p)	3d (1 1/5p)	£1 p annum + 1d (2/5p) per unit	£1.24½ p annum + 1d (1 2/5p) per unit	1965 Eastern Elec £1.57½ per quarter + 3/5p per unit
3½p	4p	6p	8p	North Thames Board 11p + 47½p p qr

1931 – 40	1941 – 44	1945 – 50	1951 – 60	1961 – 70
1936 1½d (3/5p) to 2oz 1940 2½d (1p) to 2oz	1941 2½d (1p) to 2 oz	1949 3d (1½p) to 1oz	1957 3d (1 1/5p) to 1oz	1st Class 5d (2p) 2nd Class 4d (1 3/5p)

SERVICES	1915 – 20	1921 – 30
School Fees City of London	1920 £8.40 per term	1929 £30
School Fees City of London (Girls)	NOT AVAILABLE	1929 £23 max
Harrow		£216 pa
Newspapers Daily Mail	1917 1d (2/5p)	1d
Times	1918 3d (1 1/5p)	1923 2d (4/5p)

LICENCES	1915 – 20	1921 – 30
Licences (Radio & T.V.)		
Road Tax	Cars to 6½hp £2.10 to 12hp £3.15 to 16hp £4.20 plus £1 registration	1921 £6 plus £1 per hp unit plus £1 registration

PUBLIC TRANSPORT	1915 – 20	1921 – 30
Bus Fare (Paddington to Mansion House 4 mls)	4d (1 3/5p)	4d
Rail Fare (London - Manchester - 189 miles)		1928 £1.18

PRIVATE TRANSPORT	1915 – 20	1921 – 30
Petrol (average prices)	17½p (18 changes)	8p (20 changes)
A Bicycle	£6	£6
Family Car (medium size)	£200	Morris Cowley £175 2 seater Humber 12 hp £300

1931 – 40	1941 – 44	1945 – 50	1951 – 60	1961 – 70
1936 £32	1941 £32 max	1946 £38	1960 £111 max	1970 £294 max
1936 £28 max	1941 £21 max	1946 £21 max	1960 £88 max	1970 £192 max
£216 pa	£250 pa	£234 pa	£426 pa	£669 max pa
1d	1d	1d	1957 2½d (1p)	1970 6d (2½p)
2d	1942 3d (1 1/5p)	3d	1942 4d (1 3/5p)	1970 1/- (5p)

1931 – 40	1941 – 44	1945 – 50	1951 – 60	1961 – 70
1936 Radio 50p	1941 Radio £1	Radio £1	Radio TV 1956 £1 £3 1960 £1 £4	Radio TV 1965 £1.25 £5 1969 £1.50 £6 (Colour £11)
1936 £4.50 plus 75p per hp unit	1941 £7.50 plus £1.25 per hp unit	1947 £12.10	£12.10	1961 to 6ph £10.75 6-7hp £12.50 over 7hp £15 1965 £17.50 Mar 1968 £25

1931 – 40	1941 – 44	1945 – 50	1951 – 60	1961 – 70
1933 4d	4d	1947 5d (2p)	average 3p (4 changes)	average 7p (7 changes)
1937 £1.25 1940 £1.40½	£1.45	1946 £1.65½ 1947 £1.92½	1952 £1.30 1960 £1.97	Oct 1970 £3.20

1931 – 40	1941 – 44	1945 – 50	1951 – 60	1961 – 70
8p (21 changes) including 4p tax	10½p (no changes) tax 4p	11½p (10 changes) 1950 tax 7½p	21p (32 changes) 1960 tax 12p	25p (25 changes) 1969 tax 22½p
£6		£12	£20	£30
1938 Austin 12 saloon £235		Morris Oxford £546 1947 Austin 12 £597	Humber Hawk £985 1957 Austin 12 £800	1969 Ford Escort 1300 £927

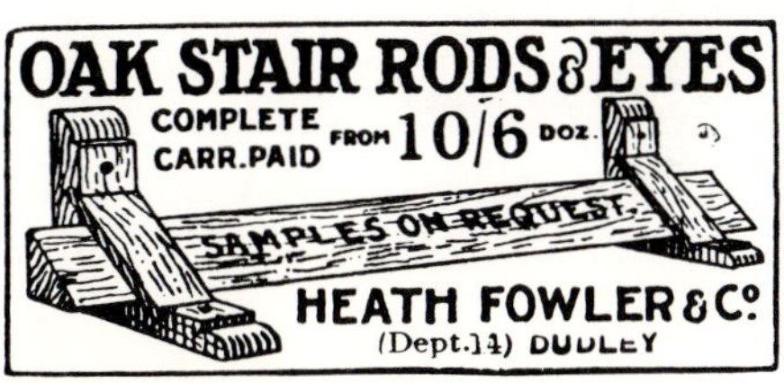

HOUSING	1915 – 20	1921 – 30
3 bedroom semi-detached	£600	£600

INCOME	1915 – 20	1921 – 30
Skilled male	£5	£5
Unskilled male	£4	£4
State Retirement Pension	25p age 70	25p age 70

INCOME TAX in the £	26p	22p

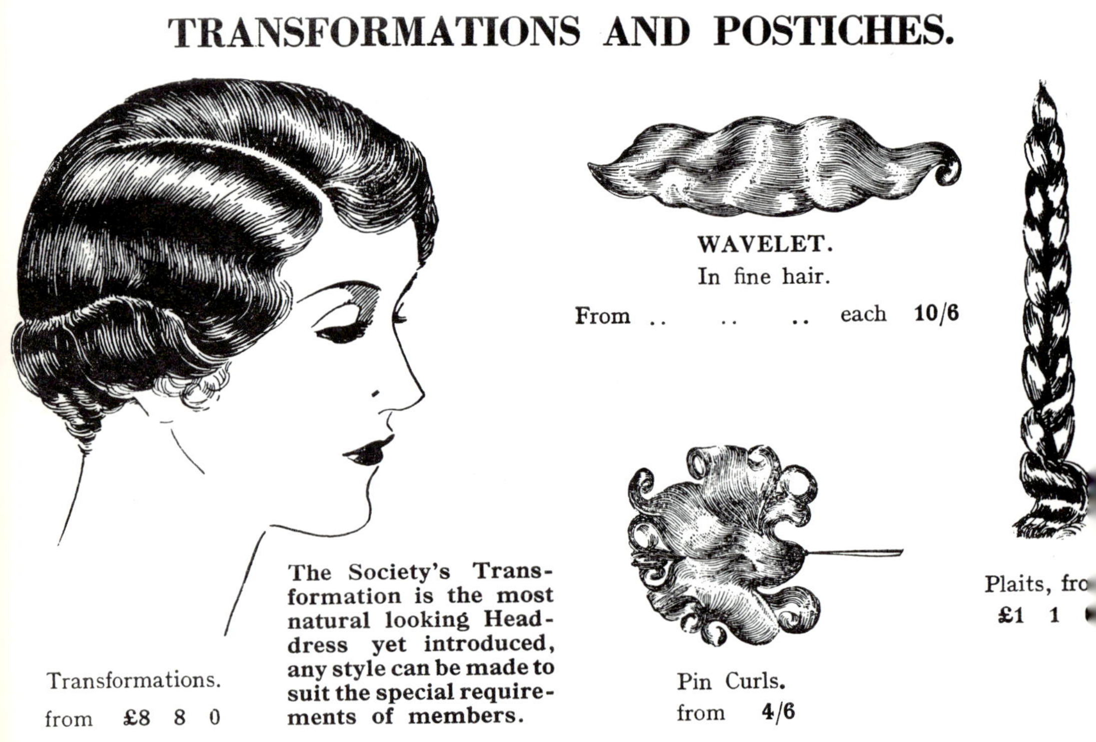

The cost of transforming the hairstyle in the early thirties

1931 – 40	1941 – 44	1945 – 50	1951 – 60	1961 – 70
£750 (provinces £650)	£800	£2,200	£2,750	London £6,000 Provinces £4,500

1931 – 40	1941 – 44	1945 – 50	1951 – 60	1961 – 70
£5	£5	£6.50	£11	£20
£4	£4	£5	£7	£13
1936 50p (men at 65 women at 60)	50p	£1.30 (S) £2.10(M)	6.9.51 £1.50 (S) £2.50 (M) 30.1.58 £2.50 (S) £4.00 (M)	6.4.61 £2.87½ (S) £4.62½ (M) 6.11.69 £5.00 (S) £8.10 (M)

24p	50p	46p	45p	40¼p

(S) - single (M) - married

Combined hand-hearse and bier cost £32 in 1933

CLOTHING

baby's complete layette *£1.75*
boy's all-wool pullovers *97½p*
boy's jersey suits *£1.12½*
dress materials
– Luvisca striped patterns *20p per yard*
– plain shades *22½p per yard*
girl's 3-piece knitwear sets *£6.30*
ladies' coats
– British moleskin from *£145*
– natural musquash from *£49*
– Persian lamb from *£83*
ladies' sets 3-piece knitwear set *£7.87½*
woollen stockinette jumper suit *£4.75*
maternity corsets *75p*
maternity skirts *50p*

COST OF FIRST EDITIONS

Jeffery Farnol Sir John Dering (1923) *37½p*
J B Priestley The Good Companions (1929) *52½p*
Wells Men like Gods (1923) *37½p*
Christina Alberta's Father (1925) *37½p*
The world of William Clissold *37½p* 3 vols *£6.30*
P G Wodehouse Leave it to Psmith (1923) *37½p*
Sam the Sudden (1925) *37½p*

DRINK

spirits
– brandy *55½p per bottle*
– gin 55p per bottle
– rum *60p per bottle*

FURNISHINGS

BEDROM (Waring and Gillow 1923)
4ft 6in oak bedstead *£7.50*
rush seat chairs *£1.25 each*
3ft dressing table *£11.50*
4ft 6in tallboy, oak *£21*
folding towel airer *£1.62½*
4ft gent's wardrobe *£29.97½*
3ft 6in washstand *£6.12½*
DINING ROOM
(Bowman Bros Camden Town, 1923)
oak bureau, 2ft 6in *£12.15*
8 chairs, hide backs *£3.15 each*
oak shaped front sideboard 5ft *£29.15*
suite, complete, cottage type, with dresser *£30*
oak draw-leaf table, 4¼x3½ft *£17.15*

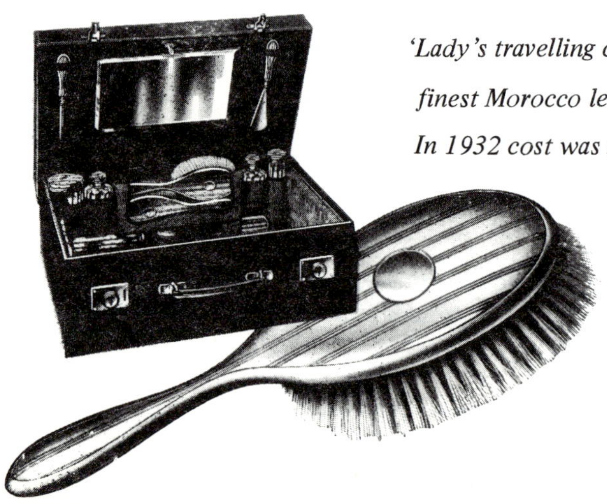

'Lady's travelling case of finest Morocco leather'. In 1932 cost was £25

LOUNGE
armchairs
–lady's *£4.25*
– gent's *£4.50*
chesterfield, upholstered, spring back and seat *£6.75*

HOUSE AND GARDEN
billiard tables 4¼ftx2¼ft *£7.75*
6¼x3¼ft *£12.50*, 8¼x4¼ft *£21.50*
casement cloths *15p per yard*
compactom clothing cabinet, inner space 4¼x1ft 7 in *£31.70*
cork lino *11p per yard*
cornice poles *15p, 24p and 37½p per foot* according to diameter including all fittings
garage 15x9ft *£30.50*
garden arches
– Perfecta, one arch *£1*
– pergola with 4 arches *£4*
– top bar 25ft run *£1.87½*
gramophone to wind up *£7.85*
greenhouses, portable 9x7ft *£20.95*, 10x7ft *£24.50*, 12x8ft *£31*
mangle, Brayknawt super chain drive *£9.45*
oak parquet flooring
27½p per square yard
piano, household *£50*
radio, 5-valve set *£20*
headphones *£1*
rug wool black *14½p per lb*
– coloured *16p per lb*
stair rods and eyes, oak, with fittings from *52½p per dozen*
tool cupboard fitted with tools *£2.37½*
wall fire with surround in briquettes *£11.55*

INCOME
cook-general *£52 per annum*
General *£44 per annum*
BEA pilot *£450 per annum*
London turner *£3.15 per week*
shorthand typist *£3.95 per week*

A luxury settee and bed combined in 1923 was £7.75

PERSONAL
wooden golf club *72½p*,
golf balls *£1 per dozen*
'Nyto kills nits and all head vermin, *2d (4/5p) per packet, 3for 5d (2p) post free.* Sold at Taylor's Drug Stores'
stylo pen *12½p*

SERVICES
Cleaning and proofing golf jackets
cleaning *27½p*, proofing *37½p*
suits cleaning *42½p*
proofing *62½p*,
costume cleaning *37½p*
proofing *60p*,
evening cloaks *47½p*
proofing 62½p,
rainproof coats proofing *47½p*
Registration of letters *3d (1 1/5p)*

TRANSPORT AND HOLIDAYS
Royal Duchess afternoon cruises from Tower Pier through the London Docks adults *17½p*, children *9p*
P & O spring cruises, 1927, 12 days Norway from *£21*,
19 days Norway from *£30*
10 days Mediterranean from *£21*
New Zealand Shipping Co, 1923.
Ten ways round the world for *£250*
Hotel Constance, Lancaster Gate, 1923 Terms from *£3.67½per week, from 62½p per day, from 42½p per night* with bed and breakfast, bath and attendance.

CLOTHING AND PERSONAL

corn knife, ivory handle and 2 blades *22½p*
corn razor with ivory handle *20p*
boots, men's *52¾p*
dress materials,
– white flannel *12½p per yard*
– herringbone tweed *30p per yard*
– Macclesfield silk *45p per yard*
– chiffon velvet *64p per yard*
– printed crepe de chine *40p per yard*
dress, velvet *£12.60*
stockings, silk *35p,* cashmere *25p*
menswear
– caps *30p*
– felt hats *£1.25,*
– bowler hats *£1.25*
Onoto fountain pen *£1*
underwear, men
– silk *£1.50*
– vest *65p*
– shirt (silk) *75p*
– pants *£1.25*
– socks *20p*
women
– combinations *90p*
– knickers *40p*
– vests *65p*
– sanitary towels, soluble, *6p per dozen*

COST OF FIRST EDITIONS

J B Priestley Wonder hero (1933) *37½p*
Laburnum Grove (1933) *25p*
English journey (1934) *42½p*
They walk in the city (1936) *42½p*
H G Wells The shape of things to come (1933) *52½p*

FOOD etc

almonds *10p per lb*
biscuits digestive plain *6p per lb* gingernuts *6p per lb*. Marie *6½p per lb,* tea *6p per lb,* petit beurre *6½p per lb*
butter beans 7lb for *9p*
Bovril, 2oz jar *4½p*
cake cherry *9p per lb,* cherry, almond iced *13p per lb* Genoa *8p per lb,* Madeira *6½p per lb* Madeira almond iced *11p per lb*
Christmas puddings *10p*
cider *75p per dozen bottles* Whiteways' draught, *15p per gallon*
cigars, Havana *7p each*
flour, 7lb for *6p*
fruit, dried apricots 7lb for *25p,*
– currants and peaches 7lb for *20p,*
– prunes 7lb for *12½p*
– raisins 7lb for *16½p*
– sultanas 7lb for *23p*
hampers for school containing:
1 Dundee cake, 2 glasses potted meats, 1 tin sardines, 1 glass veal, ham and tongue; 1 bottle barley sugar drops; 1 tin Devon toffee; 1 pot strawberry jam; 1 pot marmalade; 1 gingerbread *50p post free*
1 Dundee cake, 1 box shortbread, 1 tin mixed biscuits, 1 gingerbread, 1 glass spiced beef and tongue; 2 tins sardines, 2 glasses potted meats, 1 pot strawberry jam, 1 pot blackcurrant jam, 2 pots marmalade; 1 bottle barley sugar drops; ½lb peppermint lumps; 1 tin fruit salad; 1 tin pineapple *£1 post free*
ices *25p per quart*
jams and marmalade *5p per lb*
lard *4p per lb*
macaroni *4p per lb*
meats, cooked, sliced roast *19p per lb,* sliced brawn *6p per lb* chicken roast *20p per lb* sliced York ham *18p per lb*

oatmeal, Scots 7lb for *5p*
frying oil *50p per gallon*
split peas, 7lb for *6p*
pepper, white ground *10p per lb*
rice, *1½p per lb*
sago, 7lb for *10p*
sausage, pork *6p per lb,* Royal Cambridge *6½p per lb*
semolina, 7lb for *5p*
spirits,
– brandy *70p per bottle*
– gin *55p per bottle*
– rum 60p per bottle
sweets
– acid drops and pear drops *7½p per lb*
– barley sugar *9p per lb*
– Brazils, buttered *6p per lb*
– chocolate, plain *7p per lb*
– chocolate almonds *20p per lb*
– chocolate Brazils *25p per lb*
– chocolate peppermint creams *27p per lb*
– fudge caramel *10p per lb*
tapioca *1½p per lb*
treacle – Golden Syrup *1½p per lb*
vinegar *3½p per quart*
wines, champagne *£5.60 per dozen bottles*
– Claret *£2 per dozen,* Madeira *£3 per dozen,* port *£2.50 per dozen,* sherry *£2.50 per dozen*
white *£1.75 per dozen*

HOLIDAYS AND EXCURSIONS

Greenwich Pier-Southend *15p return or single*
Greenwich Pier-Clacton *20p return 15p single*
Greenwich Pier-Felixstowe *25p return 20p single*
Atlantis Pleasure Cruises; 13 days Mediterranean, June from *£23.50* northern capitals (Norway, Iceland etc), 12 days from *£19.95,* 22 days from *£35.70*
Royal mail, 6 days Gibraltar and Morocco from *£10.50*
hotels, bed and breakfast, average charge *45p*
meals out, 3 course luncheon *10p*
Christmas dinners *17½p*
Boxing Day special dinner *10p*
fish teas *8p*

HOUSE AND GARDEN

ammonia *5p per pint*
aspirin tablets, 5 grains *5p per 100*
baby carriage *£4.20*
bath, white, plain enamel, 5ft 11in overall *£5.31* with fittings
bath bricks *12p per dozen*
bath mat, pedestal *25p*
beetle trap The Demon *6½p*
boracic acid *½p per lb*
borax *3p per lb*
carpet sweeper, Ewbank *£1.60*
cascara tablets 24 for *5p,* liquid extract 8oz for *11p*
cinder sieve 14ins 3/8in mesh *16p*
coal cauldron, all black, plain *21p*
coat hanger, plain wood with no bar *1p with bar 3p*
cod liver oil 8 oz *4p*
curb, oak 45x12ins, 3x2in thick *£2.77*
Epsom salts *4p for 8 oz*
eucalyptus oil *5p* for 3oz
firelighters *24 for 100*
garage, timber 14x8x9ft, *£10.25,* floor extra *£2.62*
gum tragacanth *3p per oz*
aluminium kettle, welded spout, wooden grip handle, 4 pints *59p,* in copper, 4 pints *79p,* in stainless steel, 4 pints *£1.49*
lawn mower, Ransome 14in *£7.12½*
lino, inlaid *20p per square yard*
carpenter's mallet, beech with 5in head *10p*
mangle, standing iron frame and wooden rollers *£5.50*
matches, *4½p* per dozen boxes
O-cedar mop with handle *25p*
omelette pan, bright steel, 10ins *11p*
pail, oak, iron-hooped *37½p*
parqueting, oak panel, ¼in thick, *6p per square foot*

perambulator *£5.25*
Rentokil, 8oz bottle *14p*
roof felting, heavy *35p* for 12 square yds
saccharine tablets *4p per 100*
sal volatile ½ pint *20p*
saws, best hand 24ins *69p,* tenon, 10ins *14p,* hacksaw, cast iron, 10ins *11p,* blades 14p per dozen
senna confection 8 oz *5½p*
serviettes, linen *£1 per dozen*
soda 7lb for *2½p*
starch *3p per lb*
stepladder, 6 treads *80p*
stove, pocket Primus in box with complete outfit *87½p*
tablecloth *75p*
toilet paper, thin perforated, *36p per dozen rolls*
vacuum cleaner, Electrolux super swallow *£18.90*
WC suite, complete *£5.42½*

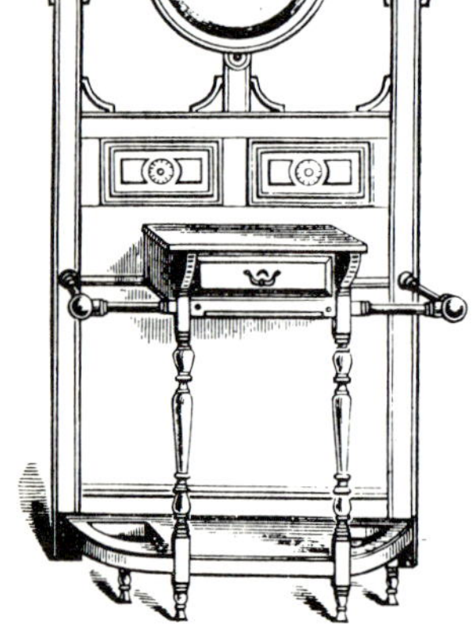

Hat and umbrella stand of 1883 in mahogany, walnut or oak. Price £8.75

washleather, 24x22ins *29p*
writing paper, cream laid 7x4½ins, *9½p per ream,* envelopes *29p per 100*
yeast tablets *12½p per 100*

INCOME

police constable *£4.12 per week*
cook – general *£55 per annum*
house parlourmaid *£48 per annum*

SPORTS AND PASTIMES

cameras, Brownie *75p, pocket* Kodak 5½x3½ *£5,* autographic Kodak *£7.50*
clarinet, 14 keys *£4.20*
cricket bat *85p*
golf balls, *65p per dozen,* clubs *65p*
greenhouse, 10x9ft *£25.50*
garden seat, 4ft teak *£4.20*
library subscription, Boots class B ordinary *37½p per annum*
netting, wire, 3½ft, 1 in mesh, 50 yard roll *£1.07*
paints, oil colours, 2-in tubes *3p,* water colours in 2-in tubes *3½p*
pencils, Venus black lead, 17 grades, *19p per dozen*
piano, Chappell *£63,* Challen baby grand, 5¼ft *£157.50*
radio, Superhet cabinet model £25, Murphy, the best model *£27*
saxophone, E-flat alto *£16.20*
tennis balls *55p per dozen,* racquets *£3.25*
tents, wedge
– 6½x5¾ft *£2.50*
– ground sheet *62½p*
– British army bell tent 13ft dia. *£7.50*
trumpet, rotary *£4.62½*
typewriter, Underwood standard *£30*

SERVICES

permanent wave, Eugene *£1.05*
registration of letters *3d (1 1/35p) 1936 4½d (1 3/5p), 1940 5½d (2 1/5p)*

ENGLISH CHIMING CLOCKS.

Estimates given for any kind of Turret Clock.

Experienced men sent to any address by arrangement

No. 98.

No. 98. Rosewood, inlaid. Height 32 inches. Lacquered and Gilt brass columns and ornaments. English Quarter Chiming Clock. London made.

Full size movement, of the best finish, with Strike and Silent attachment, and Regulating in front, Chiming and Repeating the hours and quarters on 8 and 4 Bells, and Striking hours on Cathedral Gong	£24 10 0
Ditto, on 8 bells and 5 Gongs	30 0 0

Brackets to match, from 50/0

Illustrations of other Patterns on application.

All repairs entrusted to us receive most careful attention and returned with all possible speed.

FOOD etc

FISH (1947),
– cod fillet *6p per lb*
– haddock *4p per lb*
– herring *2½p per lb*
liquors
– French brandy *£2.10 per bottle*
– cream sherry *£1.25 per bottle*
marmalade, Golden Shred *7p per lb*

FURNISHING

bedroom suite, utility *£90*

HOUSEHOLD

paraffin pressure iron *£3.42½*

INCOME

agricultural labourer (1950) *£4.70 per week*
milk salesman *£4.25per week*
London turner (1950) *£5.55 per week*

PERSONAL

6 Bathjoys *11p*
brief case, leather *£3.75*
electric razor *£10.87½*
typewriter, Empire Aristocrat portable *£20*
lady's umbrella *£3.12½*
vaseline hair tonic *12½p*

SERVICES

artificial teeth repaired from *17½p*
registration of letters *5½d (2 1/5p)*

This handsome piece of ironmongery was 'The "Perfect" refrigerator'. It was priced at £3.75 in the early thirties.

CLOTHING
dressing gown *£4.50*

FOOD etc
FISH
– white fish, filleted (1956) *12p per lb*
– herrings *5½p per lb*
– canned and bottled fish *30p per lb*

FURNISHINGS
bedroom suite *£65*
lounge suite in oak *£48,* in walnut *£65*
television chair *£10.50*

HOLIDAYS
bed and breakfast in a Bayswater hotel *£1.05*
Blackpool, full board *75p per day, £5.25 per week*
Bournemouth *£7.35 per week (summer) £5.62½ (off season)*
Barmouth *£10.50 per week* full board (1960)
Ilfracombe from *£7.87½ per week*
Balmoral, Princes Square, London *£9.45 double weekly,* including all weekend meals
Austrian Tyrol, 10 days *£17.87½,* 17 days *£21.97½*
Belgian coast, 8 days *£21.97½*
French Riviera, 8 days *£21.47*
Paris, 5 days *£11.17½*
Spain, 8 days *£20.17½*
Switzerland, 10 days *£19.37½*
Fares, tourist to Nice *£25.50 night return, £27.50 day return,* Channel Airways, Southend-Paris *£6.20 return,* Southend-Jersey *£9.60 return*

HOUSEHOLD
freezer *£60*
gramophone - record player *£14,* record cabinet *£10.50*
inlaid linoleum *35p per yard*
oil convector heater *£12*
piano, overstrung *£120;* other average *£70*
radio, portable *£12.70*
shoe polish, Nugget *2p per tin*
television, Bush 12-in *£56.70,* Murphy 21-in *£94*
typewriter, portable *£20*
washing machine *£70*

INCOME
agricultural labourer *£8* (1960)
engine cleaner *£7.47 per week*
London turner *£9.56 per week* (1960)

PERSONAL
desk lamp, adjustable *£1.50*
Ilford colour film 20 transparencies *£1.07½,* including processing
umbrella, men's *£4.50,* umbrella for day-to-day use *£2*

SERVICES
Permanent wave at hairdresser's from *£2.12½,* at home head *83p* refill *41½p*
Registration of letters *8½d (3p)*

CLOTHING AND PERSONAL
brassiere *40p*
corsets *£2.50*
lady's costume *£20*
football *£1.70*
typewriter (portable) *£25*

FOOD etc
FISH
– white filleted *19p per lb*
– herrings *9p per lb*
– salmon, canned *41p per lb*
LIQUORS, spirits,
– brandy *£3.35 per bottle,*
– gin *£2.12½ per bottle,*
– rum *£2.42½ per bottle*
wines
– red Burgundy *77½p per bottle,*
– claret *62½p per bottle*
– port, good *£1.35 per bottle*
– sherry, good *£1.25 per bottle*
marmalade *6½p per lb jar*
Nescafe *12p per* 2oz tin

SPECIAL CHRISTMAS FARE
(advertisement)
Norfolk chicken 4lb *68½p*
2lb puddings *27½p*
Stone's ginger wine *50p per bottle*

HOUSE, GARDEN etc
freezer *£60*
lawn mower, 4-stroke motor *£23.25,* superior *£40.15*
oil convector stove *£9.75*
paraffin *12p per gallon*
spin dryer *£20*
television set rental, *45p per week*
washing machine *£70*

INCOME
agricultural labourer *£11.55(1968)*
cleaners *20p per hour*
qualified engineer *£1010 per annum*
London turner *£12.87 per week*
machinist (woman) *£9 per week*
milk salesman *£13 per week (1970)*

SERVICES
haircut for men *25p*
registration of letters, *1962 9p; 1965 10p; 1966 10½p ; 1967 16½p*

TRANSPORT AND HOLIDAYS
flights to the continent, Rotterdam *£11;* Ostend *£7.40,* Channel Islands *£5 single,* Paris *£12 return*

Natural musquash fur coat. Price 49 gns, period 1927

1971 - 1978

Decimalisation (February 1971) may have had some slight effect on price rises, but the addition of a fifth of a penny here and there or even more to make a workable selling price can have been trifling compared with the economic blizzards which have shaken the country since that date.

People, according to their inclinations or their political opinions, have laid stress on different causes for Britain's misfortunes. 'Wage levels have no appreciable effect on inflation,' say the Left. 'But we cannot check inflation without controlling wage rises,' say the Right. And, in the working man's opinion, the wage question is all-important.

Other causes must, however, take their place, and some are quite as important as the wage controversy. Developing countries have become conscious of their power as suppliers of raw materials and essential foodstuffs. Of all these the foremost example is that of the oil-producing countries which in the early seventies brought about a rise in the cost of petrol and oil which not only almost doubled the motorist's bills but added indirectly to the price of everything sold in the shops.

The same could be said of many other products imported from developing countries. Rises in these prices, especially of goods used in industry, were bound to affect

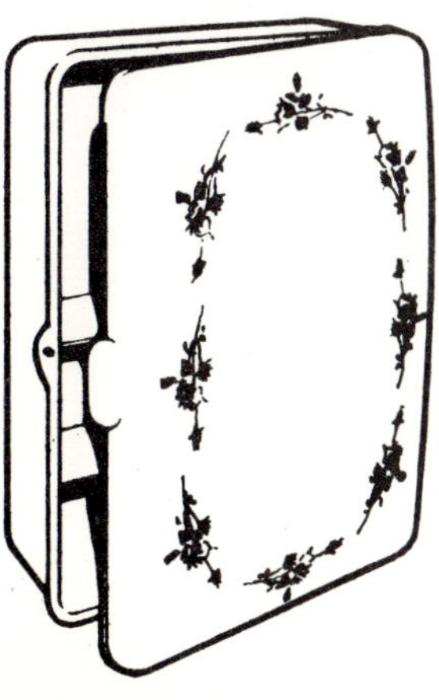

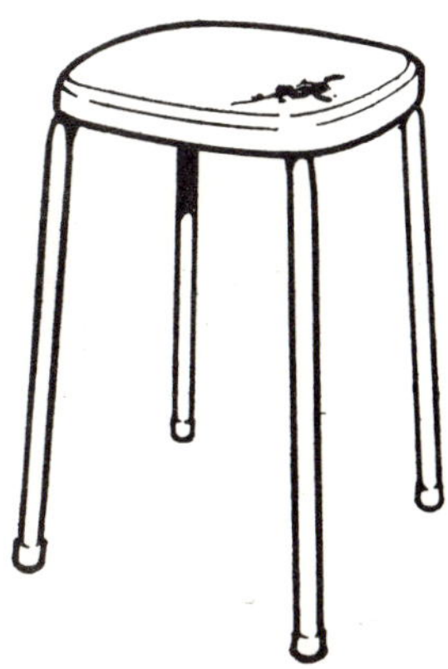

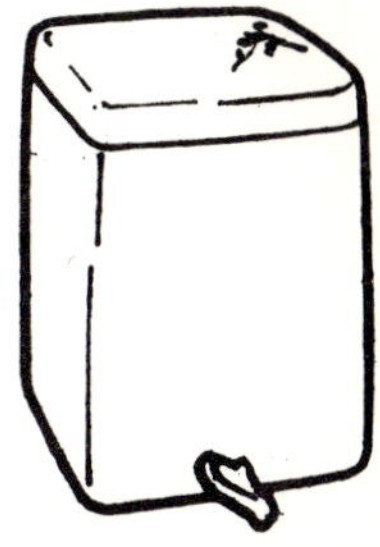

In 1970 the bathroom cabinet cost £3.47, the stool £2.83, the pedal bin £2.56

the cost of the final product of that industry. The sum total of such increases thus became an important factor in the rise in the cost of living.

Some products as for instance tea, coffee and cocoa were affected by such factors as good and bad harvests, or by higher wages paid to those who harvested the prime product. The increased prices which possibly result from these changes may in time level out prices at higher rates, but rarely do they come to be reduced to any extent once they have risen. The same in smaller measure may happen in the case of home-produced goods, especially agricultural. Potatoes became almost ten times their usual price as a result of the drought of 1976 but in 1977 when supplies again were plentiful they could be bought almost as cheaply as before. Tomatoes, apples and other fruit and vegetables fluctuate according to the season and state of the harvests, but other factors also contribute towards making them dearer or cheaper.

One of these arises from agreements made between Great Britain and other countries, and especially of recent years with the rest of the Common Market partners. We argue with them about agricultural policy, we dispute about fishing rights and the level of the green pound which was fixed when Britain joined the Community. We hear of butter mountains, dried milk mountains and wine lakes but, contrary to what we would expect, their existence does little to reduce prices in the shops. Price control there is and to some extent there has been for years, but nothing can in the end resist the overwhelming pressure of those who supply us for the returns they demand for what they produce.

In the seventies Great Britain passed into a long-lasting economic crisis which could only, it was believed, be resolved by going easy on wage claims, by buying British to keep people in employment, by increasing investment in home industries and so on. One year of restraint followed another. By 1977 inflation, which had approached 20 per cent at one time began to decrease and, by 1978 it had reached single figures.

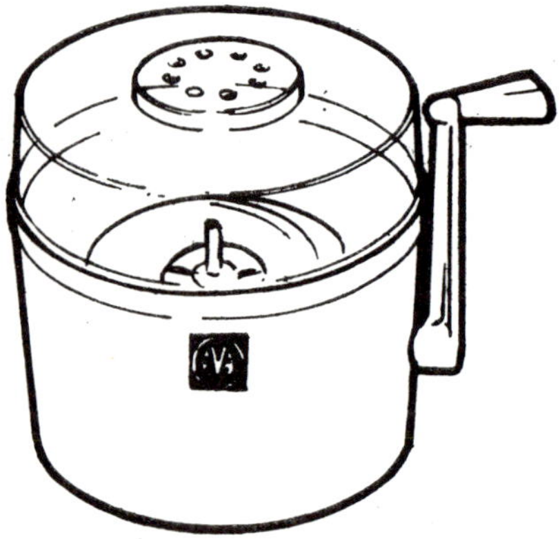

The 1970 potato peeler was in the shops for £4.59.

FOOD DRINK TOBACCO	1971	1972	1973
Apples per lb	Cooking 6.5p Dessert 10p	8p 12p	11p 12½p
Bacon per lb smoked Streaky	32p 29p	37p 26p	49p 37½p
Brandy	£3.35	£3.50	£3.75
Bread large 1¾lb loaf	9½p	10p	11½p
Butter per lb	25p	28p	22p
Cabbage per lb	4p	4½p	5p
Canned salmon per lb	52½p	58½p	68½p
Cheese (Cheddar) per lb	25p	31p	32p
Coffee 4oz instant	28½p	28½p	31p
Eggs (wide variations) per doz	22p	20p	32p
Fish White filleted per lb	27p	32p	40p
Fresh herring per lb	18½p	19p	23p
Gin	£2.50	£2.60	£2.40
Lamb (leg)	36p	41½p	54p
Lard per lb	19p	19p	23p
Liquors Beer	12p	13p	12¾p
Margarine per lb	11½p	12p	12½p
Meat Brisket	21p	26p	36p
Milk per pint	5¼p	5¼p	5½p
Pork (leg)	30p	35½p	45½p
Potatoes per lb	3½p	2½p	2½p
Rum	£2.85	£2.75	£2.75
Silverside	46p	45p	66½p
Sirloin	50p	60½p	76p
Sherry Bristol Cream	£1.32	£1.36	£1.34
Sugar per lb	8p	9½p	10p
Tea ¼lb	9p	9p	9p
Whisky	£2.57	£2.60	£2.40
Cigarettes 20 Players' Medium	31p	31½p	31½p

1974	1975	1976	1977	1978
10p 13½p	15¼p	17¾p	18¾p	23p
59p 48p	60p 52p	75p 60p	95p 82p	95p 82p
£3.99	£4.75	£5.72	£6.35	£6.35
14p	15p	21p	28p	30p
25p	29p	43p	55p	68p
8p	5p	5p	15p	15p
£1.06¼	£1.01¼	£1.50	£1.75	£1.75 (pink £1.12)
37p	42p	43p	55p	64p
36p	34½p	48p	£1.09	£1.00
36½p	40p	43p	51p	51p
50p	54p	84p	90p	£1.00
26p	27p	50p	55p	60p
£2.60	£3.00	£3.75	£4.10	£4.29
65p	68p	70p	98p	£1.20
35p	20p	26p	34p	34p
16p	21p	23¾p	26¾p	30p
18p	19½p	28p	36p	36p
49p	48½p	62p	78p	84p
5p	7p (4 changes)	9p (2 changes)	11½p	12½(Jan) 13½(Nov)
48½p	68p	74p	74p	82p
3p	3½p	17p (drought)	7p	7p
£3	£3.75	£4.40	£4.90	£4.69(Morgan)
69p	70p	72p	75p	£1.20
79½p	83p	£1.06¼	£1.35¾	£1.40
£1.75	£1.87	£1.89	£1.95	£1.99
15p	15p	23p	25p	30p
10p	10p	11p	35p	24p
£2.55	£3.40	£3.80	£4.20	£4.29
36p (5 advances)	51½p (4 advances)	56p (2 advances)	68p (2 advances)	70p

CLOTHING MEN	1971	1972	1973
Overcoat	£14	£16	£17
Shirt	£3.50	£4	£4.50
Shoes	£7	£7	£9
Suit	£22	£24	£26

WOMEN	1971	1972	1973
Coat	£18	£18	£20
Shoes	£5	£5	£6
Tights	50p	50p	50p

FURNISHING	1971	1972	1973
Bedroom bed (double with mattress)	£40	£55	£59
Blankets wool	£5	£6	£7.50
Sheets cotton	£5	£6.50	£6.50
Carpeting Axminster 36′1″	£3.20 per yd	£3.20	£4
Dining room crockery 21 pc tea set	£4.50	£5	£7
Table	£21	gate-leg – extending £24.50	£26.50
Lounge settee 4 seat convertible	£50	£50	£60
Electric cooker	£60	£72	£90
Gas cooker	£55	£65	£75
Electric fire	£25	£28	£35
Freezer	£70	£80	£95
Iron (dry)	£5	£5.50	£5.50
Refrigerator	£60	£70	£75
Sewing machine	£45	£45	£55
Vacuum cleaner (upright)	£45	£45	£45
Washing machine (twin tub)	£75	£82	£90
Typewriter	£25	£27	£32

1974	1975	1976	1977	1978
£18	£20	£26	£40	£45.00
£5	£5	£6	£6	£7.00
£9	£11	£12	£14	£19.00
£29	£36	£40	£43	£55.00

1974	1975	1976	1977	1978
£20	£25	£28	£36	£40.00
£7.50	£7.50	£9.50	£14	£17.00
50p	55p	55p	55p	60p

1974	1975	1976	1977	1978
£65	£75	£90	£110	£120.00
£10	£11	£12	£14	£15-50
£6.50	£7	£7	£8	£10.00
£4.25	£5.50	£8.50	£10	£12.00
£7	£10	£13	£14	£18.00
£40	£40	circular extending £50	£52	£70.00
£70	£75	£105	£125	£140.00
£95	£95	£120	£140	£184.00
£80	£90	£100	£110	£130.00
£38	£45	£53	£59	£70.00
£105	£120	£130	£146	£160.00
£5.50	£7	£8	£10	£12.00
£80	£85	£90	£90	£100.00
£55	£70	£75	£85	£90.00
£50	£50	£60	£65	£75.00
£90	£100	£110	£125	£140.00
£35	£40	£45	£50	£60.00

HEAT AND LIGHT	1971	1972	1973
Coal per ton	£16	£17	£18
Electricity Eastern Electricity Board	July fixed charge £1.95 per unit. 88p	July fixed charge £2.08 per unit. 92p	April fixed charge £2.21 per unit. 98p
Gas per therm North Thames Board	13p + £1.30 per qr	13¾p + £1.36 per qr	13¾p + £1.36 per qr
Paraffin per gallon	13p	14p	14p (November 16p)

SERVICES	1971	1972	1973
Postage (inland letter) minimum	1st class 3p 2nd class 2p Registration 17p	3p and 2p Registration 20p	3p and 2½p Registration 20p
School Fees City of London, pa	£315	£340	£291
City of London Girls, pa	£240	£266	£291
Harrow, pa	£759	£867	£969

NEWSPAPERS	1971	1972	1973
Daily Mail	2p (July 3p)	3p	3p
Times	5p	5p	5p (Nov 6p)

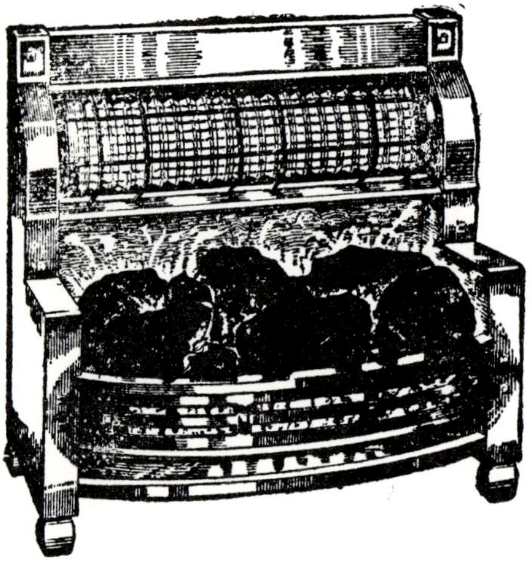

The Grafton electric fire of 1933 cost £6.10 and (opposite) the nickel plated electric iron £1.12½

1974	1975	1976	1977	1978
£22	£31.50	£43	£45	£48.00
fixed charge £2.21 per unit. 98p	fixed charge £2.21 average per unit 1.67p	fixed charge £2.21 average per unit 2.21p	Jan fixed charge £2.34 £2.60 April average per unit 2.43p	Fixed charge £2.77 average per unit £2.86
14¾p + £1.46 per qr	14¾ + £1.46 p gr Oct 1 20p to 100 therms 16½p over 100 therms + £1.25 per qr	21½p to 100 therms 16½p over 100 therms + £1.25 per qr	April 1st 22¾p per therm to 52 therms 15¼p over 52 + £2 per qr	22¾ per therm to 52 therms 15¼p over 52
16p (February 19p	30p	January 36p October 38p	46½p	46½p

1974	1975	1976	1977	1978
3½p and 3p Registration 20p	4½p and 3½p Registration 25p	8½p and 6½p Registration 25p	June 9p and 7p Registration 45p	9p and 7p Registration 45p
£411	£465	£840	£930 (£310 term)	£981.00
£366	£381	£711	£786 (£262 term)	£849–£870.00
£1100	£1270	£1530	£1800 (£600 term)	£2130

1974	1975	1976	1977	1978
Feb 4p Sept 5p	Mar 6p	Mar 7p	Feb 8p	8p Oct. 9p
6p (Sept 8p)	8p (Apl 10p)	10p (May 12p)	12p (May 15p)	15p

TRANSPORT, LICENCES	1971	1972	1973
Petrol 3 star per gallon	33½p (tax 22½p)	34¼p (2 changes) tax 22½p	36p (3 changes) tax 22½p
A bicycle	£35	£37	£39
Family car (Ford Escort)	£1067	£1178	£1228
Bus fare (Paddington - Mansion House 4 miles)	10p	13p (2 changes)	13p
Railway fare London-Manchester 180 miles	Jan £3.20 Apl £3.95	Apl £4.15 Sept £4.50	£4.50 June £4.70
T V Licence			
Black & White	£6 (July £7)	£7	£7
Colour	£11 (July £12)	£12	£12
Road tax	£25	£25	£25

HOUSING	1971	1972	1973
3 bedroom semi-detached	S.E £8,000	£9,000	£10,000
	Provinces £6,500	£7,000	£7,750

INCOME	1971	1972	1973
Agric craftsman	£16.28	£17.82	£21.45
Others	£14.80	£16.20	£19.50
Mining underground minimum	£19	£25	£27.29
Woollen unskilled	£13	£14.30	£17
Weaving overlooker	£16	£22	£25.41
State Retirement Pension	Single £6.00	£6.75	£7.75
	Married £9.70	£10.90	£12.50

INCOME TAX	38.34p in £	38¾p	30p

A bicycle stand of the early thirties. Cost 34p

1974	1975	1976	1977	1978
50½p (4 changes) VAT Apl 10% June 8% Nov 25% Tax 22½p	72p VAT 25% Tax 22½p	77½p (4 changes) VAT 12½% Tax 30p	85½p (3 changes) VAT 12% reduced Aug by 5% Tax 35p	Nov.variable c 80p
£40	£49	£52	£61.50	£63.00
£1652	£1652	£1759	£2121	£2328.08
13p	17p (2 changes)	23p (1 change)	Jan-June 26p July-Dec 30p	36p
£4.70 June £5.37 Dec £6.21	£6.21 May £7.19 Sept £8.50	£8.50 March £9.20	Jan £10.10	£11.45
£7 £12	£7 (Apl £8) £12 (Apl £18)	£8 £18	£8 (Aug £9) £18 (Aug £21)	£9.00 £21.00
£25	£40	£40	£50	£50.00

1974	1975	1976	1977	1978
£11.500 £9,000	£13,500 £9,500	£14,000 £10,000	£14,500 £10,500	£19.500 £14,750

1974	1975	1976	1977	1978
£25 £21.80 £36 £19 £27.41	£31.35 July £33.35 £28.50 Jul £30.50 £47 £21.25+£4.40* £29.66+£4.40*	£39.55 £36.50 £47 £33 £40.56	£39.55 £36.50 £47 £33+£3.55* £40.56+£3.55*	£47.30 £43.00 £47+£6*+5%† £33+£3.55*+5%† £40.56+£3.55*+ 5%+10%†
Single £10.00 Married £16.00	Apl.£11.60 Nov.£13.30 Apl.£17.50 Nov.£21.20	£13.30 £15.30 £21.20 £24.50	£15.30 £17.50 £24.50 £28.00	£17.50 £19.50 £28.00 £31.50

33p	35p	35p	33p	34p July 33p

† on gross *Cost of living supplement

BOOKCASES.

No. 4

Bookcase, with Glazed Doors to upper part, lower part enclosed with Three Doors, Three Drawers, Mahogany, Walnut, or Oak.

6 ft. wide by 7 ft. high £16 10 0

Best quality 22 10 0

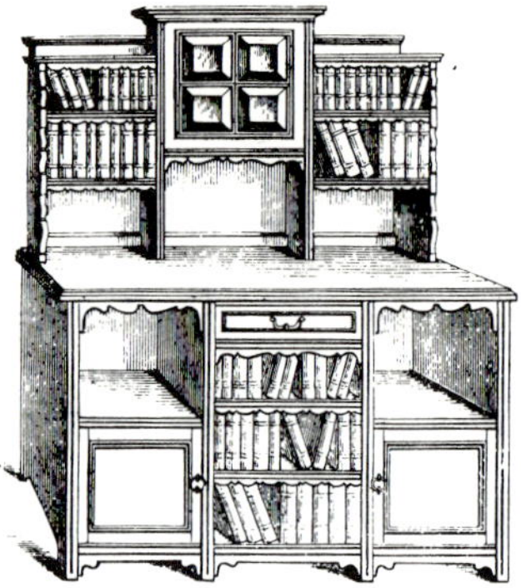

No. 5

Bookcase, top centre enclosed, with Four Bevelled Transparent Plates to Door, Cupboard at bottom on each side, Mahogany, Walnut, or Oak.

4 ft. 6 in. wide by 5 ft. 10 in. high £18 0 0

BOOKCASES.

No. 8

Bookcase, with Two Cupboards and Three Drawers, Plate Glass in back, and Gallery at top, Mahogany, Walnut, or Oak.

6 ft. 3 in. wide by 8 ft. 6 in. high £33 0 0

No. 9

Bookcase, with Four Glazed Doors to upper part, enclosed on each side at bottom with Panelled Door, Plate Glass in back, and Five Drawers, Mahogany, Walnut, or Oak.

6 ft. 6 in. wide by 9 ft. high £46 0 0

Conclusion

What is the pound worth today compared with, say the beginning of this century? Nobody knows.

In 1900 a man could keep a family of four in comfort on £2 a week, provide them with a good four or five-roomed house with 'sitting-room' and piano, good shoes and durable clothing, breakfasts and Sunday dinners with joints of good meat cooked on the living-room fire and in the side oven. And, if he was thrifty or lucky he might even have his own little barrel of ale or porter in the cellar.

BUT-

He paid no Income Tax to speak of, very little in rent or rates; he had no such home aids as gas or electric cookers, washing machines, drying cabinets and all the other articles which make housekeeping a joy-ride compared with what it once was.

His living-room was lit by gas burning a bright yellow through a Welsbach mantle, its floor covered by thin oilcloth protected in the most vulnerable places by mats and on the hearth by a large rug made at home from scraps of cloth. His bath was taken on the hearth on a Friday night in front of the living-room fire in a large zinc bath filled from the kettle; his morning wash was at the kitchen sink and his toilet was a little hut in the backyard with a scrubbed wooden seat. The little refinements of today such as toilet paper and talcum powder were almost unknown to him, and there was no such thing as an air freshener.

Because today we spend so little of our income on the sheer necessities of life and so much on what he would have considered its trimmings, it is impossible to compare the value of money today with what it was then.

For him life was rough, but if he could keep well and in employment he was comfortably off according to his standards; if not, there was no relief beyond what the parish could give, and if unemployment lasted any length of time he was lost.

Thanks to the various schemes set up by the state we are today infinitely more secure.

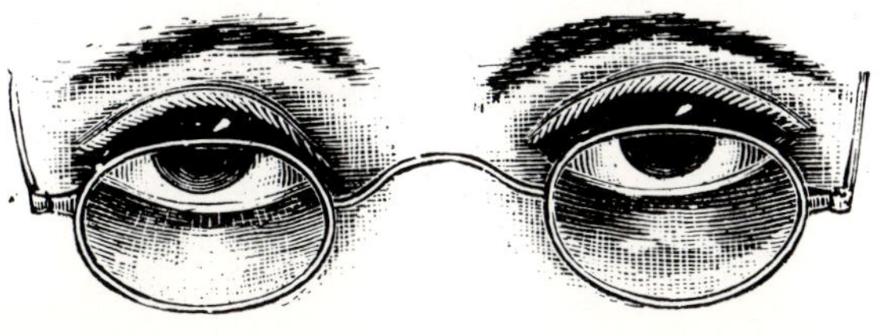

Bibliography

ANNUALS
The Annual Register
Garcke, Emil. *Manual of Electrical Undertakings* (annually until 1960)
Whitaker's Almanac

OFFICIAL PUBLICATIONS
Board of Trade, wholesale and retail prices. 1903
British Labour Statistics year books (from 1969)
Harvey, Joan M. *Sources of Statistics* 1969
Mitchell, B R and Deane, P *Abstract of British Historical statistics* 1971
Mitchell, B R and Jones, H G *Second abstract of British historical statistics* 1971
National Food Survey Committee Annual reports 1953-1975.

CATALOGUES AND LISTS
Army and Navy Stores Price List 1933-1934
The English Catalogue of Books
Gamage's Christmas Bazaar, 1913 (David and Charles)
Heal's Furniture Catalogues, 1853, 1883, 1896, 1900, 1912, 1923, 1925, 1933, 1934, (David and Charles)
Mail Order Catalogue 1971-1977. (principally those published by John Moore)
Victorian Shopping. Harrod's 1895 Catalogue (David and Charles).
Yesterday's Shopping. Catalogue of the Army and Navy Stores 1907 (David and Charles).

PERIODICALS
The Gas World
The Grocer
Which

BOOKS
Brooks, Jerone E *The mighty leaf* 1953
Chambers' Encyclopaedia *Article on Prices* (H.S.B.)
Clapham, Sir J *Economic History of Modern Britain 1887-1929.* 1951
Burnett, John *History of the Cost of Living* 1969
Davis, Dorothy *A History of Shopping* 1966
Layton, Sir W T and Crowther, G. *Introduction to the Study of Prices* 1938
London General Omnibus Co *A Hundred Years of the London Omnibus.* 1929

Monckton, H M *A History of English Ale and Beer.* 1966
Perry, George (ed) *Wheels of London*
Priest, A R and Adams, D A *Consumer Expenditure in the United Kingdom.*
Robinson, Howard *Britain's Post Office* 1953
Routh, Guy *Occupational pay and prices* 1965
Smith, J P *Some Statistics of Electricity Supply* (IMEA proceedings 1903)
Stratton, M *Agricultural Records* 1969
Willsher, Peter *The Pound in your Pocket, 1870-1970.* 1970
Young, G M *Early Victorian England.* 1934

The gentleman's compact clothing cabinet

of the early thirties, £30.95 was the cost

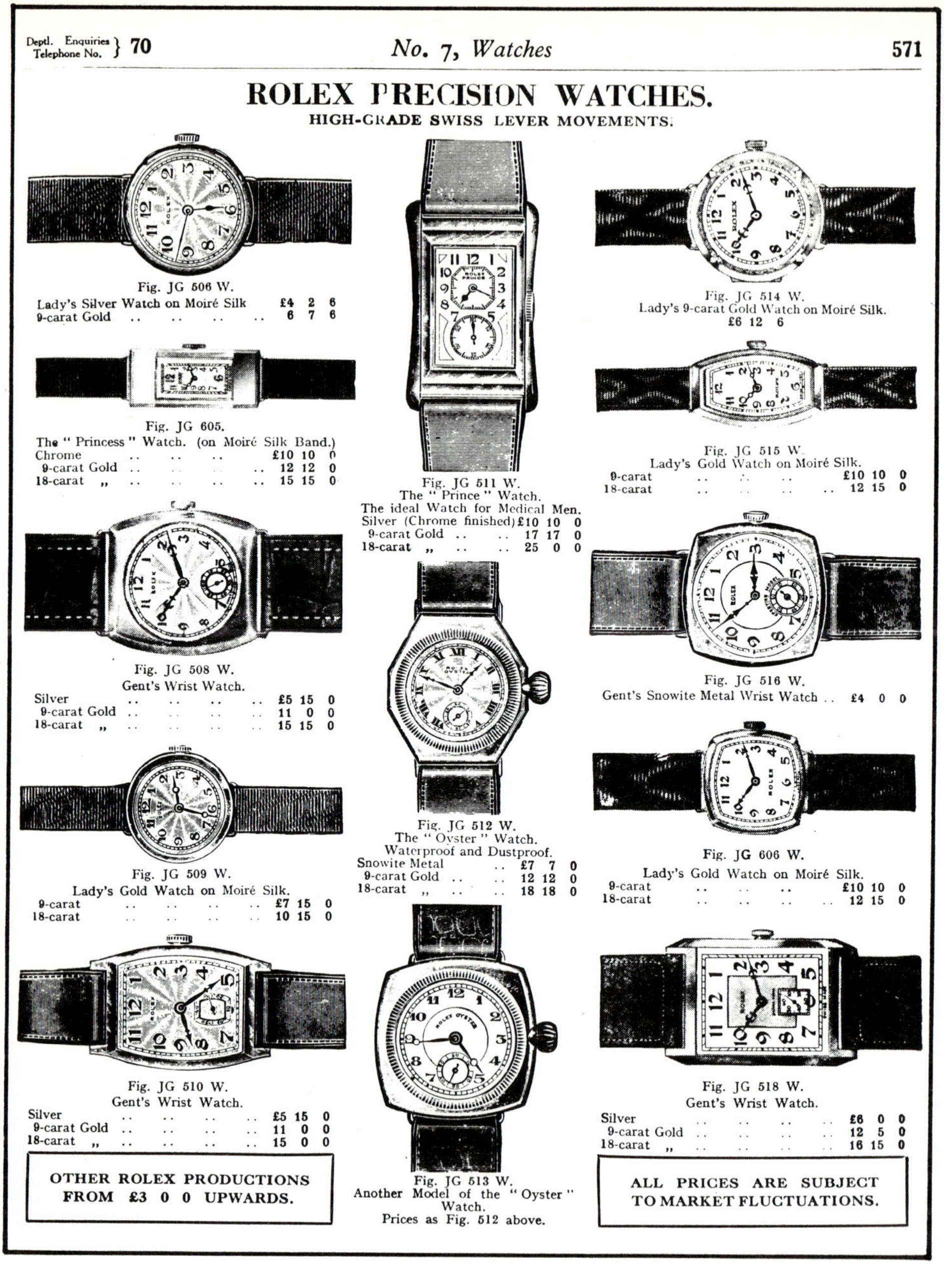

Deptl. Enquiries Telephone No. } 70 — No. 7, Watches — 571

ROLEX PRECISION WATCHES.

HIGH-GRADE SWISS LEVER MOVEMENTS.

Fig. JG 506 W.

Lady's Silver Watch on Moiré Silk	£4	2	6
9-carat Gold	6	7	6

Fig. JG 605.

The " Princess " Watch. (on Moiré Silk Band.)

Chrome	£10	10	0
9-carat Gold	12	12	0
18-carat „	15	15	0

Fig. JG 508 W.

Gent's Wrist Watch.

Silver	£5	15	0
9-carat Gold	11	0	0
18-carat „	15	15	0

Fig. JG 509 W.

Lady's Gold Watch on Moiré Silk.

9-carat	£7	15	0
18-carat	10	15	0

Fig. JG 510 W.

Gent's Wrist Watch.

Silver	£5	15	0
9-carat Gold	11	0	0
18-carat „	15	0	0

OTHER ROLEX PRODUCTIONS FROM £3 0 0 UPWARDS.

Fig. JG 511 W.

The " Prince " Watch.

The ideal Watch for Medical Men.

Silver (Chrome finished)	£10	10	0
9-carat Gold	17	17	0
18-carat „	25	0	0

Fig. JG 512 W.

The " Oyster " Watch.

Waterproof and Dustproof.

Snowite Metal ..	£7	7	0
9-carat Gold	12	12	0
18-carat „	18	18	0

Fig. JG 513 W.

Another Model of the " Oyster " Watch.

Prices as Fig. 512 above.

Fig. JG 514 W.

Lady's 9-carat Gold Watch on Moiré Silk.

£6 12 6

Fig. JG 515 W.

Lady's Gold Watch on Moiré Silk.

9-carat	£10	10	0
18-carat	12	15	0

Fig. JG 516 W.

Gent's Snowite Metal Wrist Watch .. £4 0 0

Fig. JG 606 W.

Lady's Gold Watch on Moiré Silk.

9-carat	£10	10	0
18-carat	12	15	0

Fig. JG 518 W.

Gent's Wrist Watch.

Silver	£6	0	0
9-carat Gold	12	5	0
18-carat „	16	15	0

ALL PRICES ARE SUBJECT TO MARKET FLUCTUATIONS.

The style and prices of the Rolex precision watches of the early 1930s

Index

NB (T) = to be found on the tables

C

D

E

F

G

H

I

J

K

L

M

N

O

P

Q

R

S

T

U

V

W

Y

The HMV portable gramophone of 1933 cost from £5,62½ to £8.40